Journeys through God's Word

An Introductory Course:

MARK

Leaders Guide

Mark Brighton and
Kenneth Wagener

SAINT LOUIS

Contents

Edited by Thomas J. Doyle

This publication is available in braille and in large print for the visually impaired. Write to the Library for the Blind, 1333 S. Kirkwood Rd., St. Louis, MO 63122-7295; or call 1-800-433-3954.

Scripture quotations are taken from the HOLY BIBLE: NEW INTERNATIONAL VERSION®. NIV®. Copyright © 1973, 1978, 1984 by International Bible Society. Used by permission of Zondervan Publishing House. All rights reserved.

Quotations marked NIVSB are taken from THE NIV STUDY BIBLE. Copyright 1985 by The Zondervan Corporation. Used by permission of Zondervan Publishing House.

Copyright © 1998 Concordia Publishing House
3558 South Jefferson Avenue, St. Louis, MO 63118-3968
Manufactured in the United States of America

Introduction

The study of the Bible is nothing less than an exploration into the thoughts and desires of God for ordinary people like you and me. It takes us from this hardened and selfish world into the promise of a world where God's peace, justice, and mercy will be complete.

Delving into the Bible for the first time can be somewhat intimidating. We are taken to a distant past that is full of unfamiliar customs and traditions. We must become acquainted with a nation that viewed the world differently than many people do today. And we must begin to alter some of our current definitions to grasp the full meaning of our Lord's love and compassion.

As foreign as many customs and traditions might seem to us today, we will discover that people's natures remain the same. We are trapped today—as people were centuries ago—in an imperfect world where evil and pain seem all too prevalent. We too can view the world as meaningless and without hope. But Jesus Christ came to rescue the world from its quagmire, and His deliverance continues to change our lives. Pray that the Word of God, as it comes, will begin to alter your perspective. May His promises give you rich and lasting hope and joy!

How to Use This Study

The Study Guide will direct your study of Mark. The typical lesson is divided into five parts:

1. Approaching This Study
2. An Overview
3. Working with the Text
4. Applying the Message
5. Taking the Message Home

"Approaching This Study" is intended to whet the reader's appetite for the topics at hand. It leads participants into the world of the New Testament while summarizing the issues to be examined. "An Overview" summarizes the textual material used in each lesson. Before the text is examined in detail, it is viewed as a whole, allowing participants to "see the forest" before "exploring the trees." "Working with the Text" draws participants into deeper biblical study, encouraging them to discover the gems of universal truth that lie in the details of God's Word. When questions appear difficult or unclear, the Leaders Guide provides a doorway to the answers. "Applying the Message" leads participants from the recorded Word of God to its possible application in our present lives. It helps participants more fully realize the implications of God's Word for the daily experience of a Christian. Finally, "Taking the Message Home" invites participants to continue their scriptural meditation at home. Suggestions are given for personal reflection, for preview of the following lesson, and for private study of topics raised by the lesson. The study of God's Word will be greatly enhanced by those actively pursuing the suggestions offered in this section.

Each lesson includes some "trivia" that is intended to spark interest and generate additional discussion. This can be used to develop inquisitiveness and enthusiasm about related issues ripe for exploration.

A glossary is provided at the end of the Study Guide. Because a study of the Bible will lead participants to language that may occasionally seem foreign and difficult, the glossary will make participants more comfortable with unfamiliar terms, phrases, and customs. The glossary will help them understand biblical concepts such as love and grace, whose definitions may differ from current definitions.

The Bible study also incorporates easy-to-read charts and maps that will aid participants in their understanding of biblical geography and chronology. These should be referred to frequently as they give visual support to the context of the lessons.

Session 1

The Beginning of Jesus' Ministry

(Mark 1:1–12)

Lesson Aim

In this lesson you will examine the beginning of the gospel of Mark. Unlike the other gospel writers, who begin by telling about Jesus' background, Mark jumps immediately to the start of Jesus' ministry. There is a call to repentance from John the Baptizer, and then Christ briefly appears for His baptism before His temptation in the wilderness by the devil. Mark's sudden beginning and brief account creates an urgent tone to the beginning of his gospel. This causes us to ponder, "Are we ready for Christ's coming? Are we ready to stand before God?"

These questions are sobering. Yet while the tone of the beginning of Mark's gospel is urgent and serious, Mark emphasizes that what we are about to read concerning Jesus is "Good News." Jesus came to us so that we would always be ready to stand before God without fear and guilt, ready to enter into His heavenly kingdom.

Lesson Objectives

By the power of the Holy Spirit working through God's Word, participants will

1. define the term *Gospel;*

2. use other synoptic gospels when studying Mark's gospel;

3. describe how John the Baptizer prepared people for Jesus' ministry;

4. explain why Jesus was tempted in the wilderness and what this means for us today;

5. share what Christ's second coming means to them.

Opening Worship

Pray aloud the following prayer:

Lord Jesus Christ, You once came for baptism in the Jordan River and were proclaimed by John the Baptizer to be the true Lamb of God, who takes away the sin of the world. We thank You that You came to bear our sin. We ask that You would now graciously help us to understand what we read in the gospel of Mark and that through Your Word You would strengthen our faith in You. We ask this in Your name. Amen.

Approaching This Study

Read aloud or invite a volunteer to read aloud the opening paragraphs. This section sets the stage for the remainder of today's study.

An Overview

Read aloud Mark 1:1–12. Ask participants to describe what they learn from these verses about Jesus? about Mark's gospel? Then read aloud the "Message in Brief."

Working with the Text

Discuss each of the questions included in this section. If your class is large, you may want to assign participants to small groups so that everyone has a chance to share. At the end of a designated period of time, invite groups to share their responses to the questions.

1. *Gospel* literally means "Good News." Mark's message of good news is about Jesus Christ: through His life, death, and resurrection we receive forgiveness of sins and eternal life.

2. Mark connects the message of Isaiah with the ministry of John the Baptizer. This question and the next will help participants understand the original context of Isaiah. A map will enable participants to picture where Babylon is in relation to Israel. In these verses from Isaiah, the prophet speaks words of comfort. The rebellious people are pictured as if they have already been taken into exile and punished. Isaiah now states that the Israelites' hard service (tribulation in exile) has ended.

3. Isaiah presents his message of comfort in an image that would have at once been recognized by the Israelites. Spend a few moments sharing the following information about the Exodus with the participants.

The major salvation event for the Israelites of the Old Testament was the Exodus. God used Moses to deliver His people from slavery in Egypt. God Himself, appearing in a cloud by day and a pillar of fire by night, led the people of Israel through the wilderness to Mount Sinai, where He established them as His covenant nation. He then led them through the wilderness for 40 years to the land of Canaan. Throughout this period, God delivered His people through many mighty acts.

Isaiah uses this family image to speak comfort to the Israelites who would be taken into exile. There will be a new exodus. The glory of the Lord will again be revealed and the people will again be delivered from slavery and oppression. God would again redeem His people. *Redeem* means to buy a slave freedom. The term refers to how God would ultimately free His people from the slavery of sin by purchasing their freedom from sin and death with the blood of Jesus shed on the cross.

4. The Israelites did indeed return from exile. But the prophecy of Isaiah extended beyond the return from Babylon to a time when God Himself would come and deliver His people from slavery to sin and death, their greatest enemies. Mark identifies John the Baptizer as the voice spoken of in Isaiah.

Some important things we learn about John from the other gospels is that his parents were Zechariah, a priest, and Elizabeth, a relative of Mary, the mother of Jesus. God had announced through the angel Gabriel that John would be a great prophet, sharing the same spirit and power of another great prophet of the Old Testament, Elijah. Like Elijah in days of old, John would turn the hearts of the Israelites back to God.

Some participants may ask question about Mark 1:2 and the connection of John the Baptizer to Elijah the prophet. Mark 1:2 is a quotation ~~of~~ from Malachi 3:1. There Malachi prophesies that a "messenger" will precede the coming of the Lord to prepare the way for Him. Malachi in the next chapter identifies this person as "the prophet Elijah" (Malachi 4:5). Jesus Himself clarifies the connection in Matthew 11:7–15. There He explained that John the Baptizer was Elijah, not come back to life, but sharing his prophetic power and ministry (Matthew 11:14).

John called people to repent. Those who confessed their sins were baptized by John in the Jordan River. John also clearly stated that one who was greater was coming who would baptize the people of God with the Holy Spirit and fire (Matthew 3:11–12). In this way John prepared the hearts and minds for the coming of Jesus, about whom He was speaking.

Encourage participants to make connections between the return from exile (and also the Exodus) and the coming of Christ. In the Old Testament, the people of God were enslaved to a foreign nation. John reminds us of our slavery to sin. God Himself came to redeem His people from slavery in Egypt, and He also caused their return from exile in Babylon. Jesus, God's only Son, came to redeem His people from the slavery of sin. In the Old Testament God brought His people to the Promised Land from Egypt and brought them back to their homeland from Babylon. Jesus brings us into our eternal and glorious home in heaven.

5. Take a few moments to share some other important details about the birth of Jesus. From the other gospels we learn that Jesus was born of the Virgin Mary, who was betrothed to Joseph. God was Jesus' true Father. Jesus was born in Bethlehem, thus fulfilling prophecy. Matthew tells about the visit of the Magi, and Luke about the shepherds. Jesus was raised in Nazareth, a town in Galilee. Luke tells about the boy Jesus in the temple. Then the gospel writers are silent about Jesus until His baptism.

6. Allow participants time to answer these questions. To the human eye it might appear as if Jesus is also repenting of sin. John himself, knowing who Jesus was, hesitated to baptize Him (Matthew 3:13–15). Jesus, however, did not come for baptism because of His own sin. Rather, Jesus came to take the place of sinful people and to take the sin of the world upon Himself (John 1:29; 1 Corinthians 5:21)

We also learn from His baptism that Jesus is God's unique, only-begotten Son. The voice from heaven, God, made this proclamation as Jesus came up out of the water. Emphasize this point to participants. Make a distinction between the people of God, who are God's children by adoption, and Jesus, who was truly begotten (procreated) by God. Jesus is the only person in all of creation who is at once fully human and fully divine. As a man, Jesus could live in obedience to the Law and die on the cross. But if He was only man, His perfect life and death would apply to Himself only. Since He is also God, His blood shed on the cross atones for the sins of all people.

7. From the other gospels we learn that Jesus had fasted 40 days before being tempted by Satan. Indicate to participants that fasting was an intentional period of self-deprivation, going without any food, coupled with intensive meditation and prayer. The other gospel writers tell us what some of the temptations were: turning stones into bread; casting Himself down from the temple; and falling down to worship Satan. All these temptations were attempts by Satan to make Jesus depart from the holy will of God, either by using His divine power to satisfy His own needs (stones into bread), by side-stepping His suffering on the cross while attaining worldly power (worship Satan), or by casting doubt on the gracious care of His Father in heaven (casting Himself down from the temple).

Allow participants time to state what they have learned about Jesus from His temptation. Answers will vary. Be sure to draw attention to the following: Jesus demonstrated that He is holy and without sin. Unlike Adam in the Garden of Eden, He withstood all the attacks of Satan. Jesus also indicated what type of Messiah He had come to be—a Messiah who would humbly go to the cross rather than a leader mighty with worldly power.

8. The children of Israel had been in the wilderness 40 years at the time Moses spoke the words of Deuteronomy 8:1–5. The *NIV Self-Study Bible* has some helpful information about the similarities and differences between Jesus and the Israelites.

> This testing of Jesus (the Greek verb translated "tempted" can also be rendered "tested"), which was divinely intended, has as its primary background D[euteronomy] 8:1–5, from which Jesus also quotes in His first reply to the devil. … There Moses recalls how the Lord led the Israelites in the desert 40 years "to humble you and test you in order to know what was in your heart, whether or not you would keep His commands." Here at the beginning of His ministry Jesus is subjected to a similar test and shows Himself to be the true Israelite who lives "on every word that comes from the mouth of the Lord." (NIVSB, p. 1453)

In other words, Jesus came as the perfect representative for the people of God, facing the same trials and temptations as they, yet standing in holy obedience where the people of Israel had failed.

Applying the Message

1. Jesus is the perfect and holy Son of God. He is without sin; yet He came to bear the sins of all. He came to take the place of the people of God by bearing their sin, indicated at His baptism, and by withstanding all temptation on their behalf.

2. Repentance has two parts: *contrition* and *faith.* Contrition is the knowledge that one is sinful; it is brought through the Law and results in fear before God. When we hear the full demands of God's Law, we realize how we have failed and deserve nothing but God's punishment. Faith is trusting in God's gracious forgiveness in Christ for salvation. Repentance is essential for those who would stand before God. As Scripture says, "No one will be declared righteous in His sight by observing the law" (Romans 3:20). Only Christ, by His suffering and death in payment for our sins, enables us to stand before the judgment of God. Christ has come as our substitute and stands as our representative before God.

3. Answers will vary. Point out that confession of sin has always found a place in public worship and private devotions. In the confession of sins found in our hymnal we confess our sins of thought, word, and deed. We also confess sins of commission (the evil things we have done to break God's Law) and omission (our failure to do the good things which the Law requires). There we also confess that we are sinful by nature. In other words, we are sinful not primarily because of what we do but because of who we are. Emphasize that some people believe that people are not sinful, or at least not terribly sinful, unless they regularly and obviously break God's commandments. For this precise reason many are unwilling to admit that infants also are sinful and in need of God's grace.

4. Anything that incites God's people to sin is temptation. The passage from Hebrews indicates that Jesus was tempted in all ways as God's people are.

5. Answers to the questions will vary. Note the importance of Scripture in fighting temptations. In each case Jesus quoted and stood upon the revealed will of God in Scripture and exposed the lies of Satan. Take care not to turn Jesus merely into a great example to follow. Christ surely is our example, but He is much more than that. He is also—and more important-ly—our representative. He defeated all temptations on our behalf and is thus in the unique position to help us when we are tempted. He provides the Holy Spirit, who gives us strength to withstand temptation. He grants us forgiveness when we fall. Refer to Hebrews 4:16 and 1 Corinthians 10:13. Even when God's people repeatedly fall into sin, they are neverthe-less victorious through the forgiveness of sins won by Jesus on the cross.

6. Answers will vary. If Jeff were looking only at his own life in assessing his readiness to stand before God, then indeed he will despair. There is nothing we can do to make ourselves ready. Jeff should be encouraged to look instead to Christ when he asks this question. Those who trust in Christ for forgiveness of sins and eternal life are always ready to stand before God.

7. Even those who fall repeatedly into the same sin are victorious over sin through faith in Christ Jesus. Jesus came as their representative to with-stand all temptation. So while it is important to stand against temptation, if for no other reason than God commands it, our victory nevertheless depends not on whether we fall into sin, but whether we trust in Jesus for forgiveness when we fall.

Jeff appears to be stricken by God's Law and is terrified. This being the case, every effort should be made to remind Jeff of the Gospel of Jesus' once for all suffering and death for all sins.

Taking the Message Home

Encourage participants to complete these portions of the study during the coming week. Provide a brief amount of time at the beginning of every session for participants to ask questions or make comments about the activi-ties.

Closing Worship

Pray aloud Isaiah 40:1–5 found in "Working with the Text."

Session 2

Israel at the Time of Christ

(Mark 1:40–45; 2:13–17; 5:24–34; 7:24–30; 8:27–38; 12:13–17)

Lesson Aim

This lesson will illustrate the importance of knowing about the cultural and historical context when read we Mark's gospel. In the first section a small list of important people and places will be identified and explored. A description of each of the people and places studied in this lesson are included in the Glossary of the Study Guide. A good Bible dictionary will also assist participants if more information is desired. We will then apply what we learn about these people and places to passages from Mark's gospel. Then in the "Applying the Message" section of the lesson we will draw several applications from the insights gained in these passages.

Lesson Objectives

By the power of the Holy Spirit working through God's Word, the participants will

1. explain the importance of knowing the cultural and historical context of Mark as a tool for more clearly understanding Scripture;

2. use cultural and historical contextual clues to explain the meaning of selected passages;

3. apply that which Mark's gospel teaches to their own lives.

Opening Worship

Pray aloud the following prayer:

Lord Jesus Christ, we thank You that You were born into the very fabric of our world so that we could see how the love of God works in the lives of sinful people. We especially thank You that You have brought Your love to our lives. You have forgiven our sins and made us heirs of Your kingdom. Bless us now as we read and study the gospel of Mark. In Your name we pray. Amen.

Approaching This Study

Read aloud the opening paragraphs of this study.

An Overview

Unit Reading

Read aloud or invite volunteers to read aloud Mark 1:40–45; 2:13–17; 5:24–34; 7:24–30; 8:27–38; and 12:13–17.

The Message in Brief

Invite a volunteer to read aloud this paragraph.

Working with the Text

Groups of People

Have participants tell what they may already know about each of the groups listed. Then assign individuals or groups of participants to list three facts concerning each group of people using the information included in the Glossary of their Study Guide. Allow time for individuals or groups to share the facts with the entire class. You may wish to supplement the information shared with additional facts. Have a Bible dictionary available in case additional information about the people is desired.

Answers will vary.

1. Pharisees were (a) one religious party of the Jews, (b) who tried to keep the Law and (c) taught the Law diligently in order that people might fully obey it.

2. Priests were (a) men who served in the temple at Jerusalem, (b) offered the sacrifices, (c) and had to remain ceremonially clean.

3. Teachers of the law were specialists/teachers of Jewish ceremonial, civil, and moral laws.

4. Tax collectors (a) collected taxes for the Roman Empire (b) and earned a living by adding a percentage to the tax due the government. (c) They were hated by the Jewish people.

5. Zealots were (a) members of an ultranationalistic group, (b) similar to the Pharisees in their beliefs, (c) who were willing to murder for their beliefs.

6. Samaritans were (a) a mixed race of people descended partly from the tribes of the Northern Kingdom and partly from Gentiles who were settled in Israel during the exilic period of the Old Testament. (b) They only accepted the authority of the Pentateuch and rejected the rest of Scripture.

(c) Jewish people thought that the Samaritans, along with tax collectors and "sinners," had no place in the kingdom of God.

7. Disciples (a) followed Jesus and listened to His teachings. (b) Jesus chose 12 disciples as His apostles. (c) At the end of His earthly ministry Jesus commissioned His apostles to take the Gospel to the entire world. Later, on the road to Damascus, Jesus appeared to Paul and commissioned him also to "carry My name before the Gentiles … and before the people of Israel" (Acts 9:15).

Places of Significance

Have participants locate the places listed on a map. Then once again assign individuals or groups of participants the task of listing facts about each place. Direct participants to the Glossary to find information concerning events that took place at each location.

Allow groups or individuals to share their findings with the entire group. You may wish to supplement the information shared by the participants with additional facts.

1. Nazareth was Jesus' hometown. Jesus grew up in Nazareth, but was not well received there during His ministry.

2. Capernaum was the site of some of Jesus' early miracles and the place where Jesus called some of His disciples.

3. Jesus spent much of His early ministry around the Sea of Galilee. Jesus walked on the Sea of Galilee. The sea (more properly called a lake) supported the fishing industry of the region.

4. The Jordan River connected the Sea of Galilee to the Dead Sea. John baptized Jesus in the Jordan River.

5. During Jesus time, Samaria was the land of the Samaritans. The most direct route from Nazareth to Jerusalem led directly through Samaria. Yet most Jews would avoid that route, taking a long detour around Samaria.

6. In Old Testament times, Jerusalem was the state and religious capital of the Hebrew people, beginning with King David. In Jesus' day, Jerusalem remained the religious capital of the Jews and the focus of their political aspirations. Jesus was tried in Jerusalem and crucified just outside the city.

7. Bethlehem was the birthplace of Jesus.

The Messiah

The word *Messiah* means "Anointed One." This term was uniquely applied to the one who would come from God to save His people. Additional information concerning the Messiah is included in the Glossary.

Locations and Groups of People Found in Mark

1. Lepers were unclean. Not only could they not enter the temple, but were excluded from society. They lived in isolation in their own colonies. Notice how Mark records that Jesus "touched" the leper, something no one else would do. It may seem odd that Jesus would not want the man to tell others what He had done, but this is the first of many similar commands in Mark. Jesus did not want to reinforce the incorrect messianic expectation that He would set up an age of heaven on earth by miraculously freeing all from every kind of illness. Such an expectation left no room for the work that Jesus would accomplish on the cross. Jesus commanded the leper to go to the priest because, according to ceremonial law, only the priest could pronounce the leper clean and thus restore him to temple worship and society in general. The miracle would also be a testimony to the priests about Jesus' authority, for it was thought that only God could heal a person from leprosy.

2. See the comments above in regard to messianic expectations. In short, the Pharisees imply that Jesus cannot be from God.

3. A fact rarely commented upon is that Jesus had both a tax collector and a zealot for disciples. We are left to speculate about the interesting discussions Simon and Matthew may have had and how they may have treated one another before they met Jesus. Jesus restores sinners not only to God, but also to each other.

4. According to ceremonial law, the woman was unclean. That means she was excluded from the temple. It would also not be hard for us to imagine that for this reason she was also a social outcast, unable to have children, and unable to be married. Undoubtedly, that is why Mark records this incident while Jesus is on the way to see Jairus' daughter. Jesus gives life to two types of dead people—the physically dead, Jairus' daughter, and the walking dead, the woman, who was dead to her society and faith.

Allow people time to ponder why Jesus asked, "Who touched My clothes?" The obvious answer is that Jesus actually didn't know. But this would lead to the conclusion that Jesus was not in control of His own power. He would have healed someone unwittingly, as if He were something like a charged battery. What we know about Jesus from the gospels simply does not allow this conclusion. It is much more likely that Jesus knew what the woman had done, and yet asked the question.

Jesus' attitude here is much like God's in Genesis 3, where God knows what Adam has done, yet asks, "Where are you?" and "Did you eat of the tree?" In the Garden God graciously provides Adam and Eve the opportunity to repent. Here Jesus desires the woman to step forward so that He can assure her of His love. Had He allowed her to sneak away, she would have been physically healed but still fearful about Jesus because she, an unclean woman, had touched a holy man, probably thinking she had made Him unclean also. Jesus is not interested in merely providing a physical healing. He also desires to restore her to society, and most important, to restore her faith in God.

5. The Jews thought such people had no place in the messianic kingdom. Jesus further tests her faith, essentially calling her a "dog."

6. With the cultural and historical background in mind, this question is exposed as a trick. If Jesus had answered yes, the Pharisees would immediately discredit Him, saying He could not be the Messiah because He advocates paying taxes to the Romans. If Jesus had answered no the Herodians would report Him to the Romans and no doubt try to have Him arrested for treason, a capital offense in the Roman empire.

Applying the Message

1. Answers will vary. God's grace in Christ includes those deemed by society to be the most vile. God's people are called to proclaim and share His grace with all people.

2. Healing begins with God's grace. God brings His forgiveness in Christ to individuals (John 3:16–17) and empowers them to begin sharing that same forgiveness with each other (John 13:34–35; Matthew 18:21–22).

3. Responses will vary. It was certainly not God's will that this woman suffer. Much time could be spent here on the causes of suffering and how God's people can react to it. The point that should be stressed is that when God's people suffer, they can nevertheless trust in God's gracious love and care.

Taking the Message Home

Urge participants to complete one or more of the suggested activities. The questions in the review section are designed to help participants think not only about the messianic expectations people might have today, but how congregations might present an accurate picture of Jesus Christ.

Closing Worship

Speak aloud "God's Word Is Our Great Heritage."
> God's Word is our great heritage
> And shall be ours forever;
> To spread its light from age to age
> Shall be our chief endeavor.
> Through life it guides our way,
> In death it is our stay.
> Lord, grant, while worlds endure,
> We keep its teachings pure
> Throughout all generations.

Session 3

The Miracles of Jesus

(Mark 2:1–12; 5:1–43; 6:30–44)

Lesson Aim

In this lesson you will examine some miracles of Christ. The four miracles addressed in the study illustrate three ideas that emerge when Christ's miracles are all studied together. First, they were tangible expressions of God's mercy, love, and grace. Second they demonstrated Jesus' unique authority and identity as God's Savior. Third, they called people to place their faith in Jesus as their Savior.

Lesson Objectives

By the power of the Holy Spirit working through God's Word, participants will

1. explain how Jesus' miracles point to his unique authority and power to save;
2. evaluate modern accounts of miracles;
3. affirm that Jesus answers every prayer offered in His name and promises to provide for all His people's needs.

Opening Worship

Read aloud the following stanzas from the Epiphany hymn, "Songs of Thankfulness and Praise."

Songs of thankfulness and praise, Jesus, Lord, to Thee we raise;
Manifested by the star To the sages from afar,
Branch of royal David's stem In Thy birth at Bethlehem:
Anthems be to Thee addressed, God in flesh made manifest.

Manifest in making whole Palsied limbs and fainting soul;
Manifest in valiant fight, Quelling all the devil's might;
Manifest in gracious will, Ever bringing good from ill;
Anthems be to Thee addressed, God in flesh made manifest.

Then pray aloud:

Dear Jesus, when we read about Your miracles, we are amazed by Your gracious power and thankful for Your love and grace. Thank You especially that You have performed a miracle within each of us present by creating in our hearts faith in You and love for You. Grant that we might always trust firmly in Your saving power. In Your name we pray. Amen.

Approaching This Study

Read aloud or invite volunteers to read aloud the opening paragraphs in the Study Guide. Then examine the chart. Point out that the gospel writers did not all record the same miracles. Only the feeding of the five thousand is found in all four gospels. Point out that 17 of Christ's miracles involve cures of bodily illnesses, such as blindness, paralysis, or leprosy. Nine are miracles over forces of nature, 6 are exorcisms, and on 3 occasions Jesus brought people back to life. Not all of Christ's miracles are recorded in the gospels (John 20:30; 21:25).

An Overview

Unit Reading

Have volunteers read aloud the three sections. Invite the other participants to jot down what these sections tell us about Jesus and His ministry as they listen to the passages. Then spend a few moments inviting participants to share their reactions with the group.

The Message in Brief

Read this section aloud and inform participants that what we will learn from these four miracles is evident similarly in the other miracles of Christ.

Working with the Text

1. This miracle occurs in a crowded house. Though the house is not identified in the text, it is natural to assume that it was the home of Peter and Andrew, where Jesus had stayed previously. Roofs at this time were flat, often comprising another dwelling space of a home. It would not be uncommon to sit on the roof in the cool of the day. When Jesus saw the paralytic, He responded by forgiving his sins. Though on the surface Jesus' statement may have seemed irrelevant, in fact sickness and sin are connected in many Old Testament passages. Likewise, healing and forgiveness are interrelated. See Psalm 41:4. Allow participants to speculate at to whether or not they thought the paralytic was disappointed. The discussion may lead to an analysis about his most serious problem—his sin. Far more important than temporal maladies is spiritual death.

2. The teachers of the Law thought Jesus' words were inappropriate. They thought He had blasphemed God. In its broad sense, blasphemy is a word or deed whereby someone directly affronts the honor of God. In a narrower sense, and in the sense of the text, it is dishonoring God by appropriating God's honor to oneself. That is, the teachers of the Law thought Jesus blasphemed by doing something which only God could do; He forgave the man's sins.

Make sure the participants understand this crucial point. Share this or some equivalent analogy: If you were to be robbed, it would be inappropriate, indeed impossible, for anyone to forgive the robber except you. Your neighbor cannot forgive the robber. Neither can the police or a judge and jury. Only the victim has the right to forgive. Sins, by definition, are committed against God. Therefore, only God can forgive sins. To strengthen the point, ask them to make a distinction between Jesus' direct forgiveness of sins and the forgiveness of sins which a pastor announces to the congregation in a worship service. A pastor does not forgive sins on his own authority but "in the stead and by the command of my Lord Jesus Christ." Blasphemy was punishable in levitical law by death (Leviticus 24:16). The criticism of the teachers is a denial of Jesus' divine authority.

3. The healing of the paralyzed man, besides being a direct act of mercy, becomes a challenge to the teachers of the Law, and to all gathered, to accept Jesus' uniquely divine authority. Jesus affirms the claims about His divine nature.

4. W. Foerster has written, "In most of the stories of possession what is at issue is not merely sickness but a destruction and distortion of the divine likeness of man according to creation. The center of personality, the volitional and active ego, is impaired by alien powers which seek to ruin the man and sometimes drive him to self-destruction. The ego is so impaired that the spirits speak through him." To the human eye, the symptoms of demon possession are similar to what many today would call psychological illness, and some scholars in fact suggest that the demon-possessed of the gospels were actually only mentally ill. But this contradicts Christ's own statements about demon possession. Moreover, the manner by which Jesus healed this particular man clearly demands that his symptoms were caused by the enslaving presence of demons.

5. The evil spirits are aware of Jesus' identity. Some scholars suggest that the demons, by invoking Christ's name, attempt to exert control inasmuch as the naming of a person was a sign of one's authority over that person. Notice also that the demons surprisingly invoke God's protection before Jesus. This along with the posture of the possessed man point to the demon's great fear before Christ's authority.

Scholars make various conjectures about why Jesus would allow the demons to enter the herd of pigs. Of course, pigs were considered unclean animals by the Israelites and their presence points to the fact that this was a Gentile region. In allowing the demons to go elsewhere, Jesus indicates that the time for final judgment upon Satan and his evil angels has not yet come (cf., Revelation 20:10). Moreover, the destruction of the pigs is an obvious indication to all present of the demons' intention.

6. It may seem surprising that the people would ask Jesus to leave. It seems unlikely that the sudden loss of the pigs was their primary concern. It is more likely that they recognized in Jesus a divine power and, not having faith, they were afraid. The reaction of the people in that region thus comprises a subtle and provocative counterpoint about the nature and scope of evil. A possessed man is set free, the people who were not possessed remain enslaved in fear. Mark wants us to understand that those who have no faith in Christ are in this respect like the evil angels and Satan, who fear Christ's authority.

Such a reaction on the part of the people is evidence of the extent to which sin will blind people. See John 11:45ff., where after hearing how Jesus brought Lazarus back to life, the Sanhedrin concludes that Jesus must be killed. Also in Luke 16:31, Jesus states in the parable, "If they do not listen to Moses and the Prophets, they will not be convinced even if someone rises from the dead." Mark 3:22 also gives evidence to this blindness. See also 1 Corinthians 2:14–15. Only the believing eye (the eye of faith) sees and receives the blessings of Christ. The man who had been demon-possessed was such a person. Unlike other places in the gospel (1:44 for example), Jesus tells this man to report all that the Lord had done for him. The difference is accounted for by the Gentile character of the region. These Gentiles would not be swept away by the inappropriate messianic expectations held by the Jews.

7. When Jairus heard that his daughter had died, Jesus told him to not be afraid and to simply believe. As with Lazarus, Jesus calls people to have complete faith in the most difficult of circumstances, and despite what they see with their eyes and hear with their ears they are to believe in the power of Christ to save.

8. Professional mourners were normally present at the funerals of prominent citizens, and thus their artificial and formalistic wailing immediately turns not to hope, but to laughter at Christ's words. To "fall asleep" in Jesus' culture could be taken in one of two ways, either as natural sleep or as a euphemism for death. The gospel writers want us to understand, along with the people of the house, that Jesus' words should be taken in this second sense, and not that the girl was comatose. Luke states that when Jesus called the girl to rise, her spirit, which had departed in death, returned. Jesus' command that they say nothing about this incident is probably due to the volatile and incorrect messianic expectations of the Jews.

9–12. This miracle is better understood when the connotations of "shepherd" and "wilderness" are kept in mind. Ask the participants what they would think about if you told a story about a picnic in July, where people served hot dogs, fried chicken, apple pie, and watermelon. Mom was there and you had fireworks. Without mentioning the term, you would have reminded your audience of our national heritage. So also when the Jews heard stories of wilderness and shepherds, they would be thinking about the messianic kingdom. See Numbers 15–17 and Ezekiel 34. This is precisely what Jesus wanted His disciples to think, the idea reinforced by the amount of leftover food. Since the number 12 represents the people of God, the leftovers amount to saying, "Jesus provides for all of God's people." The miracle, besides being an act of mercy for a hungry crowd, is a statement about Christ's identity as the Messiah.

Applying the Message

1. Allow people time to respond. The miracles of Christ fulfill three purposes. (a) They are tangible evidence of God's mercy and love for people and His desire to save. Thus, they are not so much ends in themselves since they support the teachings of Christ. (b) They point to the identity and authority of Christ, both to His divine nature and His messianic office. Only God can give life to the dead or cast out demons. (c) They call people to trust in Christ. Particularly with Jairus' daughter and the feeding of the five thousand, both Jesus' words and deeds demanded faith. The people who asked Jesus to leave after He cast out the demons had no faith and were left in their fear. Faith in Christ is primary and places a person in a position to receive God's healing.

The working of miracles is listed among the spiritual gifts. God uses His people to perform them according to His purposes when and where He wishes. Inasmuch as spiritual gifts are given for the continuance of Christ's work on earth through His people, we should expect miracles today to serve the same purposes. They support the teachings of the church as tangible evidence of God's mercy and love, they point to the authority of the church's teaching, and they call people to place their faith in Christ.

2. The clear teaching of Scripture is that Satan can and does use miracles to deceive. Thus, a miracle in and of itself is subject to interpretation. Where miracles undermine the clear teachings of Scripture or lead people away from Christ, they are counterfeit. Where they clearly and directly serve the Gospel, call people to faith in Christ, and conform to the revealed truths of God's Word, they may be assumed to be from God.

3. Allow people to respond. Lead participants to understand that the proclamation of the Gospel and the administration of the Sacraments are how God extends His mercy and saving power to the lives of people. A child

20

baptized at the altar is no less a miracle than the raising of Jairus' daughter. Lead people to understand that their everyday and "un-miraculous" words and deeds can demonstrate God's grace and love to others.

4. This question is designed to answer the error of "faith healers" who insist that the lack of miracles are due to a lack of faith and who appear to invoke "the name of Jesus" as if it were a magic formula. In fact, those who have a strong faith in Christ do not demand miracles. They do not need them. See Luke 11:29ff. At other times it is God's purpose to allow His people to suffer so that their faith will be strengthened. See 1 Peter 1:6–7.

The name *Jesus* means "the LORD saves." Praying for something "in the name of Jesus" therefore includes praying for those things which contribute to our salvation and that Jesus' will will be accomplished in our lives. Jesus promises to grant all such requests. Asking in the name of Jesus for things detrimental to salvation is to ask for a contradiction, and such prayers are not granted.

5. Answers will vary. Refer to the many comments above. Ellen should first of all be commended for her trust in God, but should also be gently reminded that God uses suffering to accomplish His gracious purposes. Ellen should be reminded that God also uses physicians to heal people. Ellen could also be reminded that through faith she had received healing from sin and will receive the gift of eternal life.

Taking the Message Home

Encourage participants to complete the sections under "Taking the Message Home."

Closing Worship

Read John 20:30–31: "Jesus did many other miraculous signs in the presence of His disciples, which are not recorded in this book. But these are written that you may believe that Jesus is the Christ, the Son of God, and that by believing you may have life in His name."

Then pray: Lord Jesus, we thank You for Your saving power. Grant, we pray, that when we suffer hardship, sickness, or loss we never doubt You. During such times make our faith grow ever stronger until You take us to be with You in Your glorious kingdom. We ask this in Your name. Amen.

Session 4

The Parables of Jesus

(Mark 4:1–34)

Lesson Aim

At this point of the study we will begin to look at the teachings of Jesus. This lesson will deal with His parables. Mark has fewer parables than Matthew and Luke, but those found in Mark 4 nicely introduce this area of Jesus' teaching ministry.

Lesson Objectives

By the power of the Holy Spirit working through God's Word, participants will

1. define *parable*;
2. summarize Jesus' explanation for why He spoke in parables;
3. interpret parables;
4. affirm the power of God's Word and the Gospel in the lives of God's people.

Opening Worship

Sing or read the following stanza from "Grant, Holy Ghost, that We Behold."

> Your living Word shine in our heart
> And to a new life win us.
> With seed of light implant the start
> Of Christ-like deeds within us.
> Help us uproot what is impure,
> And while faith's fruits in us mature,
> Prepare us for Your harvest.

(Text copyright © 1982 by Concordia Publishing House. All rights reserved.)

Then pray: Lord Jesus Christ, we ask Your blessings as we read and study Your Word. Graciously enlighten our hearts and minds so that we will understand what we read today. May Your teachings be ever rooted in our lives so that our faith and love for You grow ever stronger. We ask this in Your name. Amen.

Approaching This Study

Read aloud or invite volunteers to read aloud this section to introduce some characteristic features of Christ's teaching ministry. Then introduce the concept of parables. Do not spend too much time trying to explain precisely what a parable is because this issue will be addressed as part of the lesson. Rather, scan the chart to illustrate the types of parables Jesus used.

An Overview

Unit Reading

Have a volunteer read the appointed portion from Mark's gospel. Then take a few moments to discuss what parables are found there. Look particularly at verses 21–25. Ask how many parables are contained in this part of Mark where parables are defined also as enigmatic sayings. Depending on the scope of what we mean by "parable," this section contains four to six parables.

The Message in Brief

Read aloud or invite a volunteer to read aloud this section. Inform participants that through an examination of these parables, we will also learn special concerns for interpreting others, as well as why Jesus taught in parables.

Working with the Text

1. Many see the main point of the parable of the sower being the differences in the types of soil, using each to expand upon the morals of reading God's Word and the pitfalls of life that would steal that Word from us. While not denying that certain of these elements are found in the parable, the parable is best interpreted in light of the opposition Christ and His followers have encountered to this point in Mark's gospel. Jesus was criticized at almost every turn in the previous two chapters. He was accused of blasphemy (2:7), criticized for eating with "sinners" and tax collectors (2:16), questioned because His disciples did not fast (2:18), and accused of breaking the Sabbath (2:24 and 3:2). The Pharisees began to make plans to kill Jesus (3:6). They accused Him of being in league with Beelzebub (4:22). When told in this context, the emphasis of the parable is not so much the moral imperatives of reading and meditating upon God's Word as the power of God's Word to grow in a hostile environment. That is, the most important point of the parable is not the differences in the soil but the power of the seed. Such is the emphasis also of the parables of the growing seed and the mustard seed, the other parables found in this chapter.

2. Help people understand that we are at least two steps removed from these stories. They were told in the first century. We live at the threshhold of the 21st century. They were told in a Middle Eastern context, we live in a Western world. The result is that we often do not see, or misinterpret, significant details that Jesus' contemporaries would have noted. For example, if we told a story about a family having a ham dinner, we would still know very little about the family. Jesus' contemporaries, upon hearing such a story, would immediately understand that this was a Gentile family because pigs were considered religiously unclean. While participants cannot transport themselves back in time and live for a while in Palestine, help them understand the importance of commentaries and Bible dictionaries to fill in the cultural background for parables.

Before the parable is read again, remind participants of important cultural details. Seed was scattered by hand. On the surface it may appear that the sower in the parable is being careless with his seed inasmuch as some is lost to seemingly less than fertile conditions. But scholars have pointed out that in Palestinian culture, sowing comes before plowing. We should probably imagine that paths crossed fallow fields. Farmers would intentionally scatter seed on these paths with the intention of plowing them under. Thorns, which would lay in the fallow land, would not be detected until they began to grow with the good seed. Likewise, the farmer is not carelessly scattering seed among rocky crags. Rather, we should probably imagine the presence of limestone under a thin layer of topsoil.

In an ancient Middle Eastern environment, a 30-, 60-, or 100-fold harvest would have been bountiful. The last amount in particular was abnormally large. Finally, the word *harvest*, like wilderness and shepherd of previous lessons, would bring with it religious associations. In the Old Testament it was a common image of God's final judgment and the arrival of God's glorious kingdom (Joel 3:13ff.).

After reading the parable again, remind participants that parables are not be taken as allegories, where each item of the story stands for something else, but instead should be interpreted naturally in its cultural context. Generally, though there may be several points of contact between a parable and divine truth, a central emphasis will stand out for all parables. Ask the participants to describe that emphasis in a sentence.

3. Some participants may have heard this parable explained so many times that they take its meaning for granted. But those who have heard it for the first time may have felt much like the disciples. Since parables are illustrations and not direct propositions of heavenly reality, they were at times confusing to Jesus' contemporaries. But Jesus in the verses that follow gave an entirely different and more fundamental reason why people did not understand them. God's kingdom is a mystery (the sense of the original Greek) to those who are not part of it. These mysteries, or secrets, about God's kingdom are proclaimed to all, but cannot be understood by those on the outside. The next series of questions explores this issue.

4. The secret is that God's kingdom comes in Christ. Through Christ and His blood shed on the cross come God's riches (Colossians 1:25–27), His forgiveness, redemption, wisdom, and understanding (Ephesians 1:7–9). Those who have not the Spirit of God do not understand or accept that these riches of God's kingdom come only through Christ (1 Corinthians 2:6–10 and 2:14). Those "on the outside" have no faith in Christ, and their hearts and minds remain hardened against the Word of God. Verse 12 might be misunderstood to mean that Jesus spoke in parables because He did not want such people to understand the kingdom of God. However, a better translation of the Greek would be, "But to those on the outside everything is said in parables and the result is that they are ever seeing but never perceiving, and ever hearing but never understanding; otherwise they might turn and be forgiven." (In the Greek this is a *hina* clause of result, which is common in the New Testament.) Part of Jesus' ministry, like that of Isaiah, from which this quotation comes (Isaiah 6:9ff.), was to expose the hardhearted rebellion caused by sin and to bring people to repentance. When the sinful heart, by God's grace, turns to faith in Christ, the Holy Spirit enlightens both heart and mind and unfolds the mysteries of the riches of God's kingdom. Those who reject Christ remain in ignorance, and that ignorance is a form of divine judgment upon their rebellion.

The parables thus have a puzzling quality to sinful people because they convey truths that are understood and believed only through the enlightening work of the Holy Spirit. To those who come in faith to Christ, all things are explained (Mark 4:34).

5. Allow participants some time to revise their previous sentence. The main point of the parable is that in spite of all opposition, God's Gospel Word bountifully grows among sinful people, making them part of God's kingdom.

6. In these verses Jesus summons people to understand the secrets of the Kingdom. Much as a lamp is brought not to be hidden under a bowl or bed, Jesus did not come to hide the kingdom of God, but to proclaim it to all. In Christ, God both reveals and ushers in that Kingdom. That which is hidden to the sinful heart is meant by God in Christ to be disclosed. Jesus' call for people who have ears to hear is a call to faith.

The two aphorisms in this context would mean the measure by which a person comes to Christ will be the measure by which he receives. If one comes in faith, he will be given more by God's grace through that faith. Whoever has faith will be given more, such as understanding, life, forgiveness—in fact all the blessings of God's kingdom both now and completely in eternity. Whoever does not have faith, even what little life and understanding he has now will be ultimately taken away. Both these aphorisms, like the parable of the sower, look forward to the final judgment.

7. The parable of the growing seed emphasizes the power of God's kingdom. In the parable, the seed grows in spite of the passivity of the farmer, and the harvest inevitably draws near. Where the Gospel Word is proclaimed, God's kingdom mysteriously yet powerfully grows beyond all human power or activity (often in spite of human activity!). The parable of the mustard seed accents the magnitude of God's kingdom. From apparently insignificant beginnings it grows to embrace all people.

Applying the Message

1. A parable is commonly described as an earthly story, having a puzzling quality, with a heavenly meaning, which calls for a response. All these elements have been explored above.

2. This question is designed to help people evaluate congregational priorities. Answers will vary. Finally, the kingdom of God grows where the Gospel is proclaimed and the Sacraments are administered. The power of the Gospel is not limited by human weakness, small budgets, insignificant buildings, etc. All these, while important to the planning process, do not limit God's powerful grace in Christ.

3. Human words are indeed powerful. They can bring us to despair or lift us to joy. Nevertheless, human words, in comparison to God's Word, have only influential power. God's Word, on the other hand, is inherently powerful. When God speaks, things happen. When God said, "Let there be light," because of the power of His Word, it happened. God's Word is thus "living" and "active" (Hebrews 4:12).

Therefore, reading Scripture is not like reading other books. God's powerful Word does not merely influence life but creates life. When a pastor preaches a sermon, the goal is not merely to influence hearts and minds, as if the pastor where delivering a motivational speech to a team during halftime at a football game. Rather, it is the pastor's prayer that through the exposition of that Word God will powerfully change lives, bring people to repentance, and create saving faith. In the corporate confession of sins, when the pastor pronounces forgiveness of sins in the name of Christ, because it is God's Word, forgiveness happens.

4. See various comments above. It is a great comfort to trust in the power of God's Word when facing persecution or adversity. Lead participants to make applications or provide examples.

Taking the Message Home

Encourage participants to complete the sections under "Taking the Message Home."

Closing Worship

Pray: Lord Jesus Christ, You came not only to teach us about the kingdom of God, but You have also made us members of that Kingdom. Graciously lead us to regularly read and study Your Word so that by it You would continually enlighten our hearts and minds and strengthen our faith. We ask this in Your name. Amen.

Session 5

Two Great Commandments

(Mark 7:1–23; 12:28–34)

Lesson Aim

This lesson continues the last, where we began to look at the teachings of Jesus. Here we will examine one of the more well-known teachings of Jesus, that we should love others. The lesson will introduce the two great commandments, what it means to love God and to love others, and most important, what it means to say that "God is Love."

Lesson Objectives

By the power of the Holy Spirit working through God's Word, participants will

1. identify the two great commandments and explain how they fulfill all of God's laws;

2. confess that we are sinful, not only because of what we do but because of who we are;

3. describe the fundamental characteristics of God's divine *(agape)* love;

4. affirm that God in Christ not only gives us an example of divine love, but *is* divine love.

Opening Worship

Sing or read aloud the following stanzas of "Jesus, Your Boundless Love So True."

> Jesus, Your boundless love so true
> No thought can reach, no tongue declare;
> Unite my thankful heart to You,
> And reign without a rival there.
> Yours wholly, Yours alone I am;
> Be You alone my sacred flame.

Oh, grant that nothing in my soul
May dwell but Your pure love alone;
Oh, may Your love possess me whole,
My joy, my treasure, and my crown!
All coldness from my heart remove;
My ev'ry act, word, thought be love.

Then pray: Lord Jesus Christ, You are the perfect expression of God's love. Although we sin much and deserve nothing but judgment, You came with forgiveness, healing, and life. We pray that You instill such love for You in our hearts that we willingly serve You throughout our days. In Your name we pray. Amen!

Approaching This Study

Have a participant read this section aloud to the group. There are two common worldly misconceptions about Jesus' teaching on love. The first is to ignore or reject Jesus' high standard of love. In fact, it is a standard that is impossible for sinful humans to attain. The second—and perhaps more serious misconception, is to make Jesus' teaching into merely the great example of divine love. Of course, Jesus is a great (indeed perfect!) example, but He is more than that. He is also the perfect expression of God's love in that through Him God grants forgiveness, healing, and life.

An Overview

Unit Reading

Have participants read aloud Mark 7:1–20 and 12:28–34. Ask participants how these two texts, which occurred at different points in Christ's ministry, are related. Help them to see how they address the nature of true obedience to God's will.

The Message in Brief

Read aloud this section. Take a few moments to help participants recall what we learned about Pharisees from the second lesson.

Working with the Text

1. The immediate question from the Pharisees and other teachers of Jewish religious law was why the disciples did not ceremonially wash their hands before eating. Alongside the written Law of Moses was a vast body of oral tradition. This "tradition of the elders" comprised directives for all aspects of life and attempted to address situations about which the Law was silent, in order to regulate all of life in accord with the Law. The Pharisees held this oral tradition to be of equal authority with the written Law.

As in other areas, the pharisaical prescriptions for washing went well beyond that of the written Law. In the written Law priests were required to wash their hands and feet before entering the temple (Exodus 30:18–21). The mandate concerned not so much personal hygiene, but pointed beyond itself to ritual purity before God. Ritual washings served to remind the people of the necessity for God's cleansing from sin before they could approach God. The Law required the priests to remain ritually "clean." If they had been "defiled" in any way, that is become "unclean," there were prescribed sacrifices and washings necessary before they could resume priestly duties. The Pharisees expanded this requirement to include the necessity for ritual washing of not only the hands before eating daily food, but also to the ritual washing of other household items and for other reasons. It was thought inevitable that a person would become defiled when mixing with people in the marketplace, thus explaining the requirement for washing after going there.

Some scholars see noble intent behind this expansion of the Law. William Lane, for example, states,

> It is important to appreciate the concern to sanctify ordinary acts of life which lay behind this extension of priestly regulations to the laity. Its finest intention was the demonstration that all Israel was devoted to God and the Law, and the fulfillment of the injunction: "You shall be holy to me" (Lev. 20:26). The Pharisees were convinced that the strict discipline of human conduct was the necessary prelude to the true acknowledgment of God as sovereign. (*The Gospel according to Mark* [Grand Rapids: Eerdmans, 1974] p. 246.)

Jesus quickly pointed out two flaws with the Pharisees' mandates. It elevated human traditions to the same level as God's Word, thereby leading to situations where God's will was dishonored (explained in verses 9–13), and its legalistic approach to life with God fostered a devastating hypocrisy.

2. We have already seen in the gospel that Jesus' attitude toward those who were considered "unclean" was fundamentally at odds with the attitude of the Pharisees. Jesus was unconcerned about the "unclean" state caused by touching a leper (1:41) or by being touched by the woman with the flow of blood (5:27ff.) or eating with tax collectors (2:15ff.). Neither did He follow the pharisaical prescriptions concerning fasting (2:18f.) nor observing the Sabbath (2:23ff.).

3. On the one hand, the hypocrisy of the Pharisees and teachers of the law is apparent in they way they ask the question. This question is posed against Jesus not by those who want to enter a theological or academic debate. On the contrary, Mark has already mentioned how they had accused Jesus of being in league with Beelzebub (3:22ff.) and were already determined to kill Him (3:6). This question is posed merely as an opportunity to discredit Jesus.

On the other hand, the hypocrisy of the Pharisees becomes apparent in how their obedience to manmade traditions often ran counter to the will of God and was also devoid of faith. Sinful people can never keep God's commandments perfectly. Therefore, a legalistic approach to God, whereby it is thought that God's favor can be earned through right living, inevitably produces a devastating hypocrisy.

4. *Corban* was a technical, priestly term used to describe things that were dedicated, but not necessarily offered, to the Lord. The term was used in vows to prevent named people from using whatever was being offered. In the situation proposed by Jesus, a son who declared his property "corban" to his parents would prevent his parents from making use of the property, because over and against any claim they may have, it had been dedicated to the Lord. Yet because corban did not have to be offered, the son could continue to profit from the property. The Pharisees taught that such oaths were binding. Jesus illustrates how this human tradition could be used to break the Fourth Commandment.

5. Jesus' statements remind us that we are sinful by nature. We are sinful not primarily because of what we do, rather we are sinful because of who we are. Out of the heart come all manner of evil thoughts and intentions.

6. This section takes place in a different context from the preceding passage. The setting has shifted toward Jerusalem and Passion Week, when Mark records how opposition against Jesus mounted to a critical point. Yet the topic under consideration is related the questions of pharisaical tradition. The scribe asks Jesus which commandment, of all those in the oral and written tradition, was the most important.

7. Jesus responds with two quotations from the Old Testament. The first is from Deuteronomy 6:4–5. Verse 4 comprises the *"Shema"*—the primary confession of faith of every pious Jew from before the time of Christ. It is because the Lord is God that the Jews were to love Him with all their heart, soul, mind, and strength. The second quotation comes from Leviticus 19:18. Love for one's neighbor is an outgrowth of love for God and includes love for enemies (Luke 10:25–37).

Applying the Message

1. Take the opportunity to look at the Ten Commandments as recorded in Exodus 20:1–17. The first three commandments address our life with God and the next seven commandments address our life with our neighbor. It is common, therefore, to speak of two parts or "tables" to the commandments. The first great commandment, that we love God with all our hearts, souls, mind, and strength, summarizes the first "table" of the Ten Commandments (i.e., commandments 1 through 3). The second great Commandment, to love our neighbor as our self, summarizes the second table of the Ten Commandments (4 through 10).

2. Be sure to emphasize that the commandments not only forbid wrong behavior, but also command right behavior. See Luther's explanation for the commandments in the Catechism. Sinful people can never keep the commandments perfectly. For them the commandments serve as a reminder that they are sinful and need forgiveness.

3–4. These questions are designed to help people understand that the two great commandments are not any easier to fulfill than the Ten Commandments of the Old Testament. God's divine love includes self-sacrifice (John 3, Romans 5), forgiveness (John 3, Matthew 18), and faithfulness (1 John 3). It is directed not only at those who return our love, but also at those who are enemies (Romans 5, Luke 6).

This would be a good time to compare the Greek word for love, *agape*, with two other Greek words for love. One is *eros*, which describes an emotion, or passion, for someone or something. It give us English words such as *erotic*, because this passion describes physical desire. People can have emotional passion for a variety of things, such as a new car or clothes or food. *Philia*, another Greek word, describes the friendly relations between people who have a common bond, such as belonging to the same family or organization. It is less emotionally charged than *eros*. A problem arises when believers read how they must "love" each other and therefore think they must feel a certain way about each other (*eros*) or be friendly toward each other (*philia*). This is not the case. John 13:34–35 uses the word *agape*. While not denying the viability of right emotions and friendly relations, the heart of Christian love is self-sacrifice, forgiveness, and faithfulness. In other words, believers in Christ are not commanded to feel warm and fuzzy about each other (*eros*) nor are they commanded to organize potluck dinners (*philia*). They are called to sacrifice for each other, to forgive each other, and to remain faithful to each other (*agape*).

5. The Good News is that Jesus is the expression of God's love for us. Christ is self-sacrificing, forgiving, and faithful toward us. He died on the cross for our sin, forgives all our wrongs, and daily sends us the Holy Spirit to give us strength to love others, however imperfectly, with His divine love.

6. The distinguishing qualities of Christian love are self-sacrifice, forgiveness, and faithfulness. See comments for question 4 above. To the degree that people in a congregation sacrifice for each other and others, to the degree that they forgive each other and others, and to the degree that they are faithful to each other and others, they manifest to the world that they are Christ's disciples.

Taking the Message Home

Encourage participants to complete these activities in the coming week.

Closing Worship

As a prayer, read or sing the last to stanzas of "Jesus, Your Boundless Love So True."

This love unwearied I pursue
And dauntlessly to You aspire.
Oh, may Your love my hope renew,
Glow in my soul like heav'nly fire!
And day and night be all my care
To guard this sacred treasure there.

In suff'ring be Your love my peace,
In weakness be Your love my pow'r;
And when the storms of life shall cease,
O Jesus, in that final hour
Be then my rod and staff and guide
And draw me safely to Your side.

Session 6

A Prophet without Honor

(Mark 6:1–29)

Lesson Aim

There is an interesting arrangement of material in this section. Mark records three incidents. The first and the last show how people will reject and persecute those sent to speak God's word and these sections bracket the sending out of the Twelve. The arrangement reminds us that just as Jesus shares His ministry with His disciples, they also can expect to share His suffering, persecution, and rejection. But they draw comfort from the fact that God empowers them and promises to take care of them.

Lesson Objectives

By the power of the Holy Spirit working through God's Word, participants will

1. describe how Jesus shares His ministry with His followers;
2. acknowledge that God empowers His followers to carry on His ministry;
3. affirm how God promises to protect and bless those who suffer for the Gospel.

Opening Worship

Sing or read the following stanzas from "On Galilee's High Mountain."

The Lord, who born of Mary, Came down as man and died,
Who preached to all who listened, For us was crucified—
This Lord, our living Brother, In pow'r at God's right hand,
Has chosen us to carry His truth to ev'ry land.

And not alone to nations In faraway retreats,
But ev'rywhere I broadcast His love through crowded streets:
The lives that my life touches, However great or small—
Let them through me see Jesus, Who served and saved us all.

Then pray: Lord Jesus, our precious Savior, You have graciously chosen us to be Your followers. You desire that we share the Gospel, the good news that tells of Your love and forgiveness of sin, with others. We pray that You will make us bold in the presence of those who would ridicule or oppose us. Grant us Your blessing so that through our words and deeds people might come to know Your grace and place their faith in You. We ask this in Your name. Amen!

Approaching This Study

Read aloud this section. Draw attention to the fact that it may not at first seem as if these three episodes are related, but in fact, all have common themes that teach some important truths about Jesus, His ministry, and the ministry of His followers.

An Overview

Unit Reading

Have a volunteer read the section. Ask participants to think about the common elements of these three episodes. Take a few moments to identify these items.

The Message in Brief

Read aloud this section from the Study Guide.

Working with the Text

1. Jesus' hometown was Nazareth. The gospel writers tell us little about Jesus from His birth to the time He began His ministry, but the villagers' response in verse 3 indicates how Jesus learned the trade of Joseph, the carpenter. We also hear nothing of Joseph during the course of Jesus' ministry. Inasmuch as Jesus, the eldest son, when He was on the cross passed the care of His mother, Mary, to John, we should understand that Joseph had died prior to this time. Their taking offense at Jesus is more than an illustration of "familiarity breeds contempt." See 1 Peter 2:7–8 and Romans 9:33. Jesus is an offense to those who have no faith in Him.

2. Mark 3:20–21 indicates that even members of Jesus' own family had doubts about Him. Later, however, we are told in Acts that James, the brother of Jesus came to faith and was a leader in the New Testament church.

3. Matthew 10:34 emphasizes in stark terms how the coming of the Gospel in Jesus Christ results in division for the precise reason that ultimately light (believers) has no fellowship (things in common) with darkness (unbelievers). See 2 Corinthians 6:14. Jesus emphasizes this point through hyperbole, saying that He has come to bring a sword among family members. Jesus is not telling His followers to hate their unbelieving relatives. Rather, He is saying that if a choice has to be made between loyalty to family or loyalty to Him, loyalty to Him is the only alternative. Thus, faith in Christ becomes a cross to those who because of it become isolated from loved ones. Whoever finds his life (among unbelievers) will lose it, and whoever loses his life (for Christ) will find it. Matthew 19:29 is the Gospel side of this issue. The followers of Christ become part of the far greater family of God both now and throughout eternity in heaven.

4. Many scholars indicate that Jesus could do no miracles at Nazareth not because He lacked divine power, but because miracles must be accompanied by faith. "The performance of miracles in the absence of faith could have resulted only in the aggravation of human guilt and the hardening of men's hearts against God. The power of God which Jesus possessed could be materialized in a genuinely salutary fashion only when there was the receptivity of faith" (William Lane, *The Gospel according to Mark* [Grand Rapids: Eerdmans, 1974] p. 204). We have here a sobering reminder that as great as God's power is to save in Christ, God yet allows people to reject His grace.

5. The Greek word indicates that the disciples were sent out as representatives. With such a designation, people were to understand that when the disciples spoke and acted, it was as if Jesus Himself spoke and acted. To reject the disciples, the representatives, was to reject Jesus Himself. Thus Jesus also gives them authority to perform the same mighty acts that He Himself had done. They were sent out in pairs in accord with Jewish law (Deuteronomy 17:6). The presence of two witnesses was needed to confirm a testimony.

Jesus' prescriptions for the journey emphasizes how the disciples were to depend upon His divine care. They were to take only staff and sandals, the bare necessities for travel. Other items such as food, money, or changes of clothes were excluded. When they came to a town, they were to stay at one place. To move to a different location in the town would be a public insult to the host.

Shaking the dust off the feet reflects a custom of Jesus' day. Those who traveled to Gentile lands would carefully remove the dust which had collected upon their clothing, thus indicating their care to remain apart from the religiously unclean nature of those lands. For the disciples to shake the dust of their feet is tantamount to a rejection of a particular person or town within Israel. It is a declaration that the village is unclean, pagan, and Gentile in character.

The disciples preached in a manner similar to John the Baptist, calling people to repent. Casting out of demons was a continued confirmation that God's kingdom had come in power to the realm of evil and pointed to the ultimate victory over Satan on the cross. The disciples also anointed people with oil and healed the sick. In regard to the latter, we should understand that Jesus empowered them to perform miracles as He Himself had done. Scripture is less clear about the precise purpose for anointing the sick with oil. The New Testament references place it in connection with healing or praying for sick people (here, Luke 10:34, and James 5:14). Oil was used for medicinal purposes in the ancient Near East, but it was also used as a general cosmetic, such as when a person would anoint him or herself after bathing, and for religious purposes as a sign of God's blessing and empowering presence for a task or office. It is difficult to determine precisely whether the anointing of sick people in the New Testament refers to a purely medical use of oil or to oil as the sign of God's healing. If the former interpretation is adopted in our text, then Mark would be telling us that the disciples used ordinary means to heal people. If the latter, then they would have used oil as a visible reminder of God's healing. The context seems to encourage this latter interpretation.

6. This section illustrates the persecution imposed upon the prophets of God since Old Testament times. For some, the description of Herod and his wife, Herodias, together with their treatment of John the Baptizer, brings to mind Elijah's prophetic activity against Ahab and Jezebel in the Old Testament. Herod Antipas, son of Herod the Great, was Tetrarch of Galilee. His marriage to Herodias, his brother's wife, was forbidden by Leviticus 18:16. John had proclaimed to all the wickedness of this union and as a result had been arrested by Herod. Yet the text indicates that Herod was fascinated and at times disquieted by John and his preaching, and so he refused to kill him. Herodias, however, found an opportunity through her daughter, who after a captivating dance asked for the head of John. Jesus stated that John was a great prophet, the one spoken through Isaiah to prepare the way of the Lord (see comments under session 1). In this sense, he was the promised "Elijah" spoken of in Malachi 3:1.

Applying the Message

1. Take time to examine these passages. They present three ways of looking at the mission activity of God's people today.

Matthew 28:19–20. This passage teaches that Christ did not share His ministry only once with the Twelve, but He intended that they continue as His representatives after His ascension. Tell participants that these two verses are known as the "Great Commission," because they record the command of Christ Himself to His people, defining the activity of the church. Ask participants to identify what sorts of activities Jesus identifies for His followers in the Great Commission. The goal is to make disciples of all people. This is done by going into all the world, baptizing, and teaching. Inasmuch as this is Jesus' commission to all His followers, ask participants how they can be a part of it at home, work, or in the congregation.

Acts 1:8 includes another statement of Jesus before His ascension. His disciples, who had witnessed His teachings, miracles, the cross, and resurrection were to witness all these things throughout the world. Ask participants how this statement applies to them. A witness simply tells something about a person or event. Though we today are not eyewitnesses as the disciples, we are still witnesses of what Christ does among us. Ask participants what they might tell others about what Christ has done for them. Allow time for responses.

In 2 Corinthians 5:18–20, St. Paul states that he is an ambassador. Ask participants what this means. An ambassador is an official government representative. Ambassadors speak on behalf of a country or a king or ruler. Ask participants to identify the message that Paul, as Christ's ambassador, proclaimed. Paul shared a message of reconciliation. Reconciliation happens when two parties or individuals set aside their hostility and make peace. Paul states that God has reconciled Himself to the world in Christ. He has set aside His anger and wrath over sin in Christ. Paul's message to unbelievers is that through Christ they are reconciled to God. That is, they can put aside their fear, rebellion, anger, and mistrust of God and turn to Him in repentance and faith and thus receive Christ's forgiveness. Take time to consider how the people of God today are also "ambassadors" of God.

2. Each of the passages indicates how Jesus not only commissioned His people to carry on His work but also gives them the power and authority to do so. In John 20:22 we see how Christ gave His followers the authority to pronounce forgiveness of sins on His behalf. Connect this with the pronouncement of forgiveness in a worship service. Not only pastors declare God's grace. Every Christian has the privilege and duty to proclaim God's forgiveness to those who repent, whether at work, at school, or at home. In the first half of Acts 1:8 we see that Jesus promised His disciples the power of the Holy Spirit. You can illustrate how needful the disciples were of this power by illustrating the importance of the day of Pentecost in Acts 2. On that day the Holy Spirit transformed twelve confused, timid, and weak apostles into bold, powerful proclaimers of the Gospel. Ephesians 4:11–13 directs our attention to how Christ has given, and still gives, to His church spiritual gifts for carrying on ministry. 1 Corinthians 12 also deals with spiritual gifts. All God's people are part of the "body of Christ" and work to build up or edify the body in whatever ways the Spirit of God blesses.

3. Answers to this question will vary. The question is designed to allow participants to explore how the people of God today still face persecution, but more important, how God continues to bless and protect them. It is indeed terribly difficult to face opposition from one's own family for being a Christian. But the clear promise of Christ is that those who place their faith in Him are made part of a greater family of God throughout the earth and also throughout eternity in heaven.

Taking the Message Home

Encourage participants to complete the "Review," "Looking Ahead," and "Working Ahead" sections.

Closing Worship

Sing or read the following stanzas of "O God of Mercy, God of Light."

You sent Your Son to die for all
That our lost world might hear Your call;
Oh, hear us lest we stray and fall!
We rest our hope in You.

Teach us the lesson Jesus taught:
To feel for those His blood has bought,
That ev'ry deed and word and thought
May work a work for You.

Session 7

The Cross and the Kingdom

(Mark 8:27–38; 9:30–37; 10:32–45)

Lesson Aim

The three passion predictions in Mark 8–10 comprise the heart of Jesus' self-disclosure to His disciples. Together with the crowds, the Twelve have witnessed the power and compassion of the Master. They have seen Jesus heal the sick, feed the hungry by a miraculous provision, calm storms, and change lives. Though the disciples have recognized that Jesus is a prophet and teacher, perhaps it is not until Peter's confession that they understand who Jesus truly is: "You are the Christ" (Mark 8:29) that is, God's Messiah.

This lesson focuses on Jesus' messianic identity: He is the suffering, dying, and rising Messiah. As He teaches His disciples about His passion in Jerusalem, Jesus brings the Gospel to life—*His* life!

Lesson Objectives

By the power of the Holy Spirit working through God's Word, participants will

1. identify the three major passion predictions in the gospel according to Mark;
2. affirm the centrality of the cross in Jesus' role and mission as the Messiah;
3. demonstrate sorrow for the sin that led Jesus to the cross to die as humanity's Substitute and Savior;
4. find comfort and joy in Christ's call to follow Him as redeemed people who live in the grace and power of the cross.

Opening Worship

Sing together as your opening prayer the following stanzas of "In the Cross of Christ I Glory."

In the cross of Christ I glory,
Tow'ring o'er the wrecks of time.

All the light of sacred story
Gathers round its head sublime.

When the woes of life o'ertake me,
Hopes deceive, and fears annoy,
Never shall the cross forsake me;
Lo, it glows with peace and joy.

Approaching This Study

Though the three passion predictions are similar in both form and content, each has a distinctive context and application to the disciple's life. Moreover, Jesus reveals new information to His intimate group of followers in the course of the predictions. In Mark, it is apparent that the disciples become increasingly troubled by Jesus' statements; they often demonstrate, as if in direct opposition to the Lord's teaching, their lack of understanding and their own selfish ambition. The passion predictions, then, not only tell about Jesus' destiny in Jerusalem: the passion predictions also show disciples the nature of God's kingdom of grace and His invitation to discipleship.

Read this section from the Study Guide and ask participants to reflect on God's promises to send the Savior to His people.

An Overview

Unit Reading

As you prepare to read aloud the texts from Mark, ask participants to define success. If time permits, follow up with these questions: "What is required to be successful in work? How does our world measure success?"

Share that the passion predictions provide a radical new definition of success for God's Messiah.

The Message in Brief

Read this section from the Study Guide. If time permits, read aloud the entry on "cross" or "crucifixion" from a Bible dictionary.

Working with the Text

Peter's Confession and the First Passion Prediction and Teaching (Mark 8:27–38)

1. Jesus is the Christ, the Messiah. He is the "Anointed One," that is, the one set apart by God for a specific mission. (Those who were thus set apart by God were often anointed with oil.) As time permits, share the insights of a Bible dictionary on Christ, Messiah, and/or anoint. See the Glossary entries under *anoint* and *Christ.*

2. Jesus teaches that He will be rejected and put to death "by the elders, chief priests and teachers of the law" (8:31). The religious leaders had various motives for wanting to execute Jesus. The Pharisees viewed Him as a blasphemer and a "Law-breaker," that is, a person who did not strictly observe the mosaic Law. Later the chief priests, Herodians, and Sadducees viewed Jesus as a threat to the stability of the nation and the integrity of their rule. Yet Jesus continued His mission of preaching the Good News, healing, and restoring life in obedience to His heavenly Father's plan. For Jesus' teaching and actions that provoke opposition, see Mark 2:1–12; 2:23–3:6; 7:1–13.

3. As Jesus embarked on His ministry, Satan attempted to divert Him from His mission to redeem the world through the cross. Mark abbreviates the story of Jesus' temptation; for a full account, see either Matthew 4:1–11 or Luke 4:1–13. In a sense, Peter continues Satan's work by trying to deter Jesus from going to Jerusalem and the cross.

4. In the context of the passion prediction, "the things of God" include God's plan to save the world through the suffering, death, and resurrection of the Messiah. The Father's way for His Son is the way of sorrows, the way of the cross. "The things of men" could include anything that opposes or stands in the way of God's purpose: for example, success by means of idolatry, unfaithfulness, deception, etc. Allow participants to share their responses.

5. The life of discipleship is denying oneself and taking up one's cross to follow Jesus. Life with Christ means losing one's life for the sake of the Gospel. Encourage participants to share their insights into Jesus' words. Dietrich Bonhoeffer wrote, "When Christ calls a man to follow Him, He calls him to come and die." St. Paul describes discipleship in terms of Baptism into Christ's death and new life in His resurrection (Romans 6:1–4).

The Second Passion Prediction and Teaching (Mark 9:30–37)

1. Jesus now teaches the disciples that He will be "betrayed into the hands of men" (9:31). Jesus did not teach this truth to the crowds because He did not want any person to interfere with His destiny at Jerusalem (e.g., people may have tried to prevent Him from entering the holy city, or others may have tried to betray Him to the religious leaders). The disciples were increasingly perplexed and frightened by Jesus' teaching because He spoke of His death, His resurrection (they did not understand what it meant; see Mark 9:10), and His betrayal. The Twelve may have wondered if the betrayer was in their midst.

2. The disciples probably thought about greatness in terms of worldly power, prestige, success, wealth, and comfort (see, for example, Luke 7:18–28 and the description of ancient rulers). Encourage participants to reflect on their assumptions about greatness in today's world.

3. Jesus reverses the usual order of the world by offering a picture of the servant as the model of faith and discipleship. Instead of seeking fame or power or personal gain, Jesus' disciples seek, by the power of the Holy Spirit, to serve the Master and one another.

4. In Mark 9:36–37, a "little child" represents the humble believer in Christ, the gentle, faith-filled person who welcomes other believers and in turn is welcomed by the community of faith. A culture that values power and status above all things is not likely to welcome and receive little children with genuine regard and joy. Jesus' followers are like little children (see also Mark 10:13–16), and His church warmly embraces all who trust in Him with a child-like, humble faith.

The Third Passion Prediction and Teaching (Mark 10:32–45)

1. In His last passion prediction, Jesus specifically reveals that His suffering, death, and resurrection will occur in Jerusalem, that He will be handed over to the Gentiles, and that He will be mocked, spit on, and flogged before He is killed.

2. James and John seek power and status. They want, in a sense, to be leaders of the other disciples; they want prestige in the church and the authority to make key decisions in Jesus' absence. It is ironic that James and John make this request in the light of Jesus' own teaching about His suffering and death! Participants may want to reflect on and elaborate on human attitudes and ambition: too often what we desire is power and influence, rather than opportunities to serve others.

3. The cup represents the fate that awaits Jesus: the cross. The baptism is an allusion to His pouring out His blood at Calvary for the forgiveness of sins. At His water baptism, Jesus stands in solidarity with us and as our substitute. At the cross, Jesus is again "baptized" (in the symbolic sense of covered) with His own blood. His baptism at Calvary signifies His entire saving work.

4. In summary, Jesus teaches faith-filled service to others in His name. His disciples are different from the "great" rulers of society; the focus is always on serving, not being served. The model and the strength for a life of service is Jesus Himself. Encourage participants to share their thoughts and feelings on Mark 10:45.

Applying the Message

1. Use the following as a guide for understanding Isaiah's Servant Song as a prophecy of Christ. The words in italics refer to Christ; words in bold refer to us or to the blessings we have received through Christ.

> See, *My servant will act wisely;*
>> *He will be raised and lifted up and highly exalted.*
>
> Just as there were **many who were appalled at Him—**
>> *His appearance was so disfigured beyond that of any man*
>> and *His form marred beyond human likeness—*
>
> so *will He sprinkle many nations,*
>> and kings will shut their mouths because of Him.
>
> For what they were not told, they will see,
>> and what they have not heard, they will understand.
>
> Who has believed our message
>> and to whom has the arm of the LORD been revealed?
>
> *He grew up before Him like a tender shoot,*
>> and *like a root out of dry ground.*
>
> *He had no beauty or majesty* **to attract us to Him,**
>> nothing in His appearance that **we should desire him.**
>
> *He was despised and rejected by men,*
>> *a man of sorrows, and familiar with suffering.*
>
> Like one from whom men hide their faces
>> *He was despised,* and **we esteemed Him not.**
>
> Surely *He took up* **our infirmities**
>> *and carried* **our sorrows,**
>
> yet **we considered** *Him stricken by God,*
>> *smitten by Him, and afflicted.*
>
> But *He was pierced for* **our transgressions,**
>> *he was crushed for* **our iniquities;**
>
> *the punishment that brought* **us peace** *was upon Him,*
>> *and by His wounds* **we are healed.**
>
> **We all, like sheep, have gone astray,**
>> **each of us has turned to his own way;**
>
> and *the LORD has laid on Him*
>> **the iniquity of us all.**
>
> *He was oppressed and afflicted,*
>> *yet He did not open His mouth;*
>
> *He was led like a lamb to the slaughter,*
>> and as a sheep before her shearers is silent,
>> *so He did not open His mouth.*

By oppression and judgment He was taken away.
    And who can speak of **His descendants?**
For He was cut off from the land of the living;
    *for **the transgression of My people** He was stricken.*
He was assigned a grave with the wicked,
    and with the rich in His death,
though He had done no violence,
    nor was any deceit in His mouth.

Yet it was the Lord's *will to crush Him and cause Him to suffer,*
    and though *the* Lord *makes His life a guilt offering,*
*He will see **His offspring** and prolong His days,*
    and the will of the Lord *will prosper in His hand.*
After the suffering of His soul,
    He will see the light of life and be satisfied;
*by His knowledge My righteous servant will justify **many,***
    *and He will bear **their iniquities.***
Therefore *I will give Him a portion among the great,*
    and *He will divide the spoils with the strong,*
because *He poured out His life unto death,*
    *and was numbered with **the transgressors.***
For *He bore **the sin of many,***
    *and made intercession for **the transgressors.***

(Isaiah 52:13–53:12)

2. God's people in Christ can take comfort in knowing that God has chosen and saved us individually (as well as collectively) through the cross. Calvary is a demonstration of divine love; see John 3:16. Jesus goes willingly and deliberately to His death because He loves all people, even His enemies. One of the fierce opponents of the early Christian church, St. Paul would later write, "I have been crucified with Christ and I no longer live, but Christ lives in me. The life I live in the body, I live by faith in the Son of God, who loved me and gave Himself for me" (Galatians 2:20).

3. On the cross, Jesus became accursed—condemned—in our place. Though we deserved to be punished—condemned—because we failed to keep God's commandments, Jesus took on Himself the curse of the Law and suffered punishment in our place.

On the cross, Jesus also took our spiritual powerlessness and death and forgave all our failures, weaknesses, and sins.

4. This question helps participants to reflect on the cross as the one sure anchor for life and the compass that orients all their decisions and actions.

Taking the Message Home

Invite participants to read "Review," "Looking Ahead," and one or more of the "Working Ahead" suggestions. As you look forward to the next stories in Mark, remind participants that Jesus is the Lord who walks with His people into the future. Through Christ and in His strength, we can face, endure, and ultimately overcome all the different challenges life brings in the years ahead.

Closing Worship

Pray aloud:

Lord Jesus, what can we trust in life? What is our greatest comfort on earth? It is You, Lord. Your love is without limit. Your mercy lasts forever. Thank You for Your sacrifice on the cross. You have made us Your own and called us to follow You. Give us Your strength that in all situations we may serve You. In Your name we pray. Amen.

Session 8

The Last Days

(Mark 11:12–25; 12:1–12; 13:1–37)

Lesson Aim

In this session you will read, interpret, and understand Jesus' teachings on the fall of Jerusalem and the end of the world. The four gospels record the different ways Jesus revealed what would happen in the future: through a prophetic sign, through parables and statements in public, and through private discourse to His disciples. This subject, known as eschatology or the study of "last things," is often among the most difficult parts of Christian teaching. Jesus did not reveal everything about the events and signs of the time; He did not want His disciples to be preoccupied with dates and times. Yet Jesus did devote a portion of His last week of ministry to instructing His disciples about the fate of Jerusalem and the time before His second coming in glory. By carefully reading His words in context, we may understand the Lord's will for His people and take comfort in His promises.

Lesson Objectives

By the power of the Holy Spirit working through God's Word, participants will

1. identify the different types and contexts of Jesus' teaching: prophetic action, parable, and private discourse;

2. explain the two major themes of Jesus' eschatological teaching: the destruction of Jerusalem and the end times;

3. draw comfort from Jesus' promise to His disciples—to be present with them in times of hardship and persecution;

4. live in confident expectation, watching and waiting for the Lord's return in glory at the Last Day.

Opening Worship

Pray aloud the following prayer:

Holy Father, You reign in glory and power and truth. In Your mercy You have given us salvation through our Lord Jesus, who will come again with glory and power and truth as judge of all people. Keep us strong in faith. Sustain us in the time of trial. By Your Holy Spirit, draw us close to You, that we might stand firm to the end of life. We pray in Jesus' name. Amen.

Approaching This Study

Read aloud or invite a participant to read aloud the opening paragraphs.

An Overview

Unit Reading

Read together the passages listed in this section.

The Message in Brief

Invite a volunteer to read aloud this paragraph.

Working with the Text

The Fig Tree, the Temple, and the Vineyard (Mark 11:12–25; 12:1–12)

1. Still a distance away, Jesus notices leaves on the fig tree. But this tree, though in bloom, has no fruit. The fig tree has the appearance of bearing fruit, but in fact it has not produced fruit. Some people may think that Jesus' judgment on the fig tree is harsh (especially "because it was not the season for figs; verse 13). Yet the leaves without fruit provide an apt picture of barren religion: faith without works or works without faith. See Luke 13:6–9 and James 2:14–24 for similar themes.

2. Answers may vary as participants describe the scene in the temple courtyard. The area would have been filled with tables, benches, cages, animals, people, etc. In the process of buying and selling, many dishonest practices were likely; people would have tried to cheat visitors and foreigners, and visitors may have tried to take advantage of exchange rates and policies. At times, the exchange may have degenerated into "robbery."

3. The withering of the fig tree made a powerful impression on the disciples. They obviously recognized the power of Jesus over nature, but they also may have recognized the symbolic meaning: the temple would soon "wither" and be destroyed. In ancient writings, a story was often inserted between the beginning and ending of another story (a literary technique called a "sandwich"). The middle story, then, was framed by what happened in the outer story. The withering of the fig tree gives a picture of what will happen to Jerusalem and the temple.

48

4. In the Song of the Vineyard (Isaiah 5:1–7), the prophet portrays God as the planter and caretaker of the vineyard. God prepares the place (a "fertile hillside"; verse 1), builds a watchtower, plants the vines, and makes the winepress. But the vineyard yields "only bad fruit" (verse 2). God, in His righteous judgment, destroys the vineyard.

5. Answers may vary as participants note the connections between the owner of the vineyard and God. Jesus' parable has many similarities to Isaiah 5: the vineyard, winepress, and watchtower. In Jesus' parable, God plants and provides for the vineyard and then allows tenants—"farmers"—to work the ground. Like the owner's servants, the Old Testament prophets were abused, persecuted, and sometimes killed during their mission.

6. Answers may vary as participants characterize the tenants. The tenants kill the servants so that they need not respond to the owner in gratitude for his goodness and their blessings. The tenants kill the owner's son because he is the heir, and they think they will be next in line to inherit possess the vineyard when the son is dead. A close reading of the parable shows that the story summarizes the history of Israel and points to God's plan to send His Son to die at the hands of the tenants. Afterward, however, the tenants are punished. The vineyard is given as a gift to others.

The "Last Days" and the End of the Age (Mark 13:1–37)

1. Jesus warns first and foremost about false prophets and christs. They will claim, after Jesus has ascended to heaven, to be the Messiah. The spirit of the antichrist is "every spirit that does not acknowledge Jesus" as the Messiah sent from God (1 John 4:2–3).

Discuss how people—especially those who are not well grounded in Scripture—can be deceived by those who claim that Jesus wasn't who the Bible says He is or who claim to have special revelations from God or special knowledge of what the future holds.

2. Insurgents and soldiers in the temple, trampling the holy place and fighting God and one another, was an abomination, that is, an offense to God. The Roman army, with its vast manpower and resources, brought unprecedented distress to the people of Judea. The Jewish historian Josephus provides us with a vivid, tragic description of the war with Rome and the siege and conquest of Judea and Jerusalem.

3. In Mark 13:24–26, Jesus tells us that the natural order will be drastically changed: the sun, moon, and stars will no longer shine in the sky. He quotes the language of the Old Testament (Isaiah 13:10; 34:4) to give a concise picture of sudden and dramatic transformation of the universe. "At that time" (Mark 13:26) that is, when the final signs of the end times are evident, Jesus will return in glory. It is important to note that the final signs are linked to the end of time and Jesus' second coming. The language of the Old

Testament is, however, sometimes metaphorical, and perhaps this should not be interpreted in an absolute, literal sense.

4. Jesus means by the "lesson from the fig tree" that His disciples can see and understand the signs of nature: they know what follows what in the course of the seasons. In the same way, they can know and understand God's plan as they listen to His Word and watch carefully for the fulfillment of His promises.

Discuss how Jesus' promise that He will return and that this present, evil age will come to an end can bring us great comfort especially in times of hardship.

5. Jesus interprets His brief parable of the homeowner as an exhortation for the disciples—of all times and places—to watch for His sudden return. No one can truly know when the Master will arrive at home. A faithful servant, therefore, is always ready.

Applying the Message

1. Answers will vary on the types of hardships Jesus' disciples face today, ranging from persecution and death in some countries to ridicule and discrimination in other lands. God's people can prepare for these hardships and the Lord's return by standing firm in faith, growing in their knowledge of His Word of forgiveness, life, and salvation in Christ, praying for one another, etc.

2. Responses will vary. Many people may be frightened by circumstances in our world, but Christ walks with us through every day and every situation. St. Paul affirmed God's grace and strength as he served his fellow Christians throughout the Roman Empire. He focused on the Gospel and trusted that Christ, in whatever the future held, would bring him safely through every danger and trouble to eternal life in heaven.

3. Jesus will return in splendor. Because of His sacrificial death and triumphant resurrection, He is the Savior of the world; He is also the Lord of the universe. He is forever alive, and He is crowned with eternal power and glory, which He always uses to guide and strengthen His church. The elect are those who believe in Jesus as the promised Messiah and Savior. In His mercy, God chooses us to believe and works faith in our hearts. Answers may vary on the comfort believers have in knowing Christ will return to take us to glory in heaven.

4. Answers may vary. In general, it would be important and helpful to refer to Jesus' words: "No one knows about that day or hour, not even the angels in heaven" (Mark 13:32). God invites His people not to speculate on dates and times, but on personal preparation and participation in the mission to share the Good News with the world (Mark 13:9–11).

Taking the Message Home

Urge participants to complete one or more of the suggestions. The exercises in the review section are designed to help participants integrate into their lives the major themes of the session.

Closing Worship

Speak aloud the following prayer:

Most loving God, keep me from being overwhelmed
by the cares and busyness of this life. ...
Do not let flesh and blood overcome me,
nor the world with its brief glory deceive me,
nor the devil with all his cunning ensnare me.
Give me strength to resist, patience to endure,
and constancy to persevere in faith.
In Jesus' name. Amen.

(Adapted from *Following Christ: Prayers from Imitation of Christ in the Language of Today*, ed. by Ronald Klug [Concordia Publishing House, 1981] pp. 42–43.)

Session 9

The Passion of Christ (Part 1)

(Mark 14:12–52)

Lesson Aim

This lesson explores the first part of the passion narrative in Mark's gospel. Because the story of Jesus' Last Supper, arrest, trials, and condemnation covers two lengthy chapters, it is helpful to divide the account into two main sections and numerous episodes. Yet the passion narrative must be read as a whole; each sentence and paragraph details the fulfillment of God's ancient promises about His Son, Israel's Servant Savior, the Messiah who bears the sins of the world.

Lesson Objectives

By the power of the Holy Spirit working through God's Word, participants will

1. recognize the passion narrative as the fulfillment of Old Testament prophecy and, along with the resurrection, the climax of the gospel story;

2. confess their failures to trust, follow, and serve Christ in the midst of personal troubles and temptations;

3. affirm the authority and power of Jesus through the events of Maundy Thursday;

4. rejoice in the forgiveness the Savior showers on us through His obedient life, suffering, and death.

Opening Worship

Pray aloud the following prayer:

Merciful and eternal God, Father of humankind and our gracious Father in Christ, You sent Your Son into our world to be our Savior. You did not spare Him the pain of suffering and death but gave Him up as a sacrifice on the cross. Thank You for salvation! Thank You for life and forgiveness! Thank You for Your assurance: death is defeated and heaven is ours! By Your Holy Spirit, let us listen again to the old, old story of Jesus and His love. In His name we pray. Amen.

Approaching This Study

Read aloud or invite a participant to read aloud the opening paragraphs.

An Overview

Unit Reading

Read together the passage listed in this section.

The Message in Brief

Invite a volunteer to read aloud these paragraphs.

Working with the Text

The Lord's Supper and Jesus' Prediction of Peter's Denial (Mark 14:12–31)

1. Jesus' disciples are eager to prepare the Passover meal. Jesus instructs two of His disciples to go into Jerusalem, where a man carrying a jar of water will meet them. They are to follow him. When he enters a house, they are to ask the owner where the guest room is where the Teacher may eat the Passover with His disciples. In the large Upper Room the owner shows them, they are to prepare the Passover.

This Passover is especially important to Jesus because it is the last one He will celebrate before He fulfills the Passover by being sacrificed for the sins of the world. That the disciples found everything just as Jesus had said shows that He has all things under His authority and power.

2. In Mark 14:18 Jesus reveals that one of the Twelve will betray him. In biblical times, eating together was a sign of intimacy and fellowship. Thus it is especially poignant that Jesus' betrayer is one who shares the intimacy of table fellowship with Him (see Psalm 41:9). The disciples are saddened and shocked by Jesus' announcement and one by one say, "Surely not I?" (Mark 14:19).

3. During the Passover meal, people ate an unblemished lamb that had been sacrificed, just as during the first Passover their ancestors had eaten the lamb whose blood marked the doorframes of their houses (Exodus 12:5–8). When the angel of death saw the blood of that lamb, he passed over the house and did not kill the firstborn who lived there (Exodus 12:23). The Lord's Supper points to the sacrifice of Jesus, "our Passover lamb" (1 Corinthians 5:7), who was sacrificed that God might pass over our sins and spare us from eternal death.

Both the Passover and the Lord's Supper involve eating and drinking specific elements. The bread and the wine that Jesus designates as His body and blood are elements of the Passover meal. Just as those who ate the Passover ate the flesh of the lamb that was sacrificed for them, so those who eat the Lord's Supper eat the flesh and drink the blood of the Lamb who was sacrificed for them.

The Passover recalls and celebrates God's mighty deliverance of His people from bondage in Egypt. The Lord's Supper recalls and celebrates God's salvation of people from sin, death, and Satan through the sacrifice of His beloved Son.

4. Jesus reveals that all the disciples will abandon Him in fulfillment of Scripture (Zechariah 13:7). Jesus is the shepherd who will be struck in Zechariah's prophecy, and the sheep who will be scattered are His disciples. Jesus promises that after He has risen, He will go ahead of the disciples into Galilee.

5. Let participants share their descriptions of Peter and their views on whether he has changed in the course of his travels with Jesus. Peter "promises" not to fall away even if all the others do (Mark 14:29) and that he will never disown Jesus even if he has to die with Him (14:31). Peter's outspoken confidence inspires the other disciples to make the same "promises."

Jesus Prays and Is Arrested in Gethsemane (Mark 14:32–52)

1. On a number of occasions Mark notes Jesus' practice of praying, thus showing how integral it was to His mission and ministry. Peter, James, and John were the inner circle of Jesus' disciples who were privileged to accompany Him by themselves on two previous occasions (Mark 5:37; 9:2). Perhaps Jesus is seeking the support of these intimate followers during His time of anguish. Perhaps He wants them especially to pray for strength for the upcoming trial because all three had expressed confidence in their own abilities to follow Him no matter what the cost (see question 3 in this section in the Study Guide). He asks them to keep watch (Mark 14:34), that is, to stay awake and pray (see 14:37–38), while He prays.

2. Jesus prays to His Father that He might not have to undergo the upcoming suffering and death for the sins of the world that He knows awaits Him. Jesus' anguish is revealed by the words "My soul is overwhelmed with sorrow to the point of death" (Mark 14:34) and "Take this cup from Me" (14:36). Jesus is overwhelmed with sorrow at the prospect of drinking the cup of God's wrath (see Isaiah 51:17, 22) and thus experiencing separation from Him. Nevertheless, Jesus expresses His trust in and obedience to His heavenly Father by calling Him "Father," by acknowledging that all things are possible with Him, and by asking that God's will be done and not His own (Mark 14:36).

3. Peter, James, and John are prime examples of human pride; they placed undue confidence in their own abilities before the fact and were totally blind to how weakness and fear might determine their actions when the time actually came. Their inability to stay awake even for an hour is also a prime example of how frail human beings are.

The willing spirit that Jesus mentions in Mark 14:38 is a gift of God (Psalm 51:12). And only God can provide the strength needed by humans whose bodies also are weak to stand fast in the hour of temptation. Jesus knows the severe temptation to forsake Him that awaits His disciples, and He urges them to follow His example and "watch and pray so that [they] will not fall into temptation" (Mark 14:38). Let participants share examples that illustrate the truth of Jesus' words about the frailty of humans.

4. Judas identifies Jesus with a kiss. Discuss how the disciples would have felt betrayed by Judas. One of them (Peter according to John 18:10) responds by using his sword to cut off the ear of the high priest's servant. Jesus responds by asking why they need to arrest Him with military might when they could have seized Him at any time when He was teaching in the temple. But, as Jesus notes, it is happening this way to fulfill the Old Testament.

5. Discuss ways disciples are tempted to abandon Christ or compromise their faith as they live their lives in this world. Might and strength often characterize the way things work in this world, and against such might and strength Christians, armed only with the Word of God and with love, often seem "naked" and vulnerable. However, the ultimate victory has already been won for them by Christ, and they "fight" on the side of the almighty God of the universe, from whose love nothing in this world can separate them (Romans 8:31–39).

Applying the Message

1. Encourage participants to discuss ways the Lord's Supper has been a blessing in their lives. By celebrating the Lord's Supper, God's people proclaim to one another and to the world that Christ's body was broken on the cross and His blood was there shed that they might have forgiveness, life, and salvation.

2. Discuss the difficulty of standing up for Jesus in our world and the temptations and challenges believers face as they live for Christ.

3. Encourage participants to discuss the comfort in praying to their heavenly Father and then acknowledging that He knows best by praying that His will be done. Also discuss how it is hard for us to do that at times since we so often think we know what is best, and like Jesus in Gethsemane, we would rather not be subjected to painful experiences, even though we trust that God works out all things for our ultimate good in Christ (Romans

8:28). But we thank the Lord Jesus that because He obediently did the will of the Father and was forsaken by Him on the cross (Mark 15:34), we will never be forsaken by Him and will never have to face any difficult situation alone.

We know that it is God's will for us in Christ to remain firm in our faith unto the end that we might receive the crown of life (James 1:12; Revelation 2:10) and to live lives that bring glory to Him no matter what our circumstances (1 Peter 2:12). We rely on Him for the strength and grace so to do.

Taking the Message Home

Invite participants to read "Review," "Looking Ahead," and one or more of the "Working Ahead" suggestions. Encourage daily reflection on the passion accounts in Mark or one of the other gospels.

Closing Worship

Speak aloud the following prayer:

Help me, Lord Jesus, to rest in You
above all created things, above all health and beauty,
above all glory and honor, above all dignity and power,
above all knowledge and riches, above all joy and gladness,
above all fame and praise, above all sweetness and comfort …
above all things visible and invisible,
and above everything that is not Yourself, O my God.
In Your name, I pray. Amen.

(Adapted from *Following Christ: Prayers from Imitation of Christ in the Language of Today*, ed. Ronald Klug [Concordia Publishing House, 1981] pp. 12–14.)

Session 10

The Passion of Christ (Part 2)

(Mark 14:53–15:20)

Lesson Aim

In this session you will read about, interpret, and understand Jesus' trials before the religious leaders, Herod Antipas, and Pontius Pilate. The passion narrative has been divided into three parts in this course: Session 9 explores the events of Maundy Thursday; Session 10 focuses on Jesus' trials; and Session 11 covers the actual crucifixion and Jesus' burial. In one respect, the passion narrative must be read as a whole: each scene or unit contributes to the complete, Spirit-inspired story of Jesus' saving work. Yet to appreciate fully the details of the passion story—details that convey the depth of God's love in Christ—it is helpful to read the passion narrative slowly, deliberately, and reverently.

Lesson Objectives

By the power of the Holy Spirit working through God's Word, participants will

1. identify the six trials or hearings that Jesus suffered through;
2. confess, with Peter, their failure to confess Jesus as Lord and Savior in thoughts, words, and actions;
3. rejoice in Christ's great confession before the Sanhedrin and Pilate and His willing sacrifice on the cross for their forgiveness and life;
4. share their hope of salvation in their daily living.

Opening Worship

Pray aloud the following prayer:

Lord Jesus, in Your suffering and death You were patient and loving toward Your accusers. In humility You walked the way to Calvary and stretched out Your arms on the hard wood of the cross to be a ransom for all. We thank You for Your sacrifice. Draw us and all people to Your passion.

May we be found today and at the Last Day Your faith-filled people, trusting in Your mercy always. In Your name we pray. Amen.

Approaching This Study

Read aloud or invite a participant to read aloud the opening paragraphs.

An Overview

Unit Reading

Read together the passage listed in this section.

The Message in Brief

Invite a volunteer to read aloud this paragraph.

Working with the Text

1. Encourage participants to read about the high priest and the Sanhedrin in a Bible dictionary or another resource. In the Old Testament the high priest was a descendant of Aaron, the first high priest. The high priest, as leader of the priests, was to make sure that the priests carried out their duties. The high priest alone could enter the Most Holy Place on the Day of Atonement to make atonement for himself and the people (see Leviticus 16). In New Testament times the position of high priest was no longer hereditary and was filled by the Romans. However the high priest still carried out many of the priestly functions described in the Old Testament. And he was the presiding officer of the Sanhedrin.

The Sanhedrin, the highest governing body of the Jews in Jesus' day, consisted of three groups: the chief priests, the elders, and the teachers of the law. The Romans allowed the Sanhedrin to exercise a considerable amount of power in governing the Jewish people in both religious and civil matters. But there were some things the Sanhedrin did not have the authority to do, and executing prisoners was one of them.

2. The chief priests and the rest of the Sanhedrin have difficulty presenting credible witnesses against Jesus. Many false witnesses are presented, but their testimony does not agree (Mark 14:56–59). The religious leaders want to get rid of Jesus no matter what it takes. As would be evident to Pilate, the motive of the chief priests is envy (15:10).

3. Some of the false witnesses testify that they heard Jesus say that *He* would destroy this man-made temple (meaning Herod's temple) and in three days build another, not made by human hands. But Jesus had said to the Jews who demanded a miraculous sign from Him that if *they* destroyed this temple (meaning His body), he would raise it again in three days (referring to His resurrection from the dead). Encourage participants to cite other examples from Mark of people misunderstanding and misrepresenting Jesus.

4. Caiaphas asks Jesus, under oath, whether He is "the Christ, the Son of the Blessed One" (Mark 14:61), that is, whether He is the Messiah and the Son of God. Jesus answers that indeed He is. Then He applies two Old Testament messianic prophecies to Himself by saying that these people will see Him sitting at God's right hand and coming on the clouds of heaven (see Psalm 110:1 and Daniel 7:13–14). Upon hearing this, the high priest tears His clothes in outrage and accuses Jesus of blasphemy, of claiming for Himself the majesty and authority that belong to God alone. The Sanhedrin condemns Him to death, the penalty for blasphemy.

5. Peter keeps a low profile by sitting with the guards in the courtyard (Mark 14:54). He likely fears that the religious authorities might arrest him as well and subject him to the same treatment and sentence as Jesus.

6. One of the high priest's servant girls first recognizes Peter. The fact that Peter is a Galilean, something that would be evident from his speech, gives him away as a follower of Jesus, the Prophet from Galilee. Galilee is considered something of a backwater by many Judeans, and Peter's accusers might think Peter is an uneducated "country boy."

7. Jesus forthrightly confesses who He is in words that He knows will be used to condemn Him to death, while Peter denies any knowledge of or connection with Jesus, thus trying to avoid the possibility of death. Peter is vehement in his denials of Jesus to the point of calling down curses on himself (Mark 14:71). But he is repentant and remorseful after the rooster's crow brings Jesus' prediction of his denials to his mind, thus awakening him to what he has done.

8. Pilate's primary concern was to satisfy the crowd (Mark 15:15) and thus avoid the possibility of a riot in the pilgrim-packed Jerusalem. While Pilate recognized that Jesus had committed no crime (15:14) and that the chief priests had handed Him over out of envy (15:10), yet Pilate considered Jesus expendable and was willing to flog and crucify Him, an innocent man, in order to appease the crowd. Pilate was also concerned that one claiming to be "king of the Jews" might be viewed by his Roman superiors as a threat to Roman rule (see John 19:12).

9. Herod hopes to see Jesus perform a miracle. Pilate might have hoped that Herod would render a verdict in this case and make it unnecessary for him to do so.

10. Pilate tries to benefit from the usual custom of releasing a prisoner by trying to talk the crowd into accepting Jesus. This would allow Pilate to free Jesus, an innocent man, and keep a guilty man in prison. But the crowd demands that Barabbas, imprisoned for insurrection and murder, be released and that Jesus, the guiltless one, be crucified.

Applying the Message

1. Jesus, the agent of creation (John 1:3), gave us physical life, and then by giving Himself into death for our salvation, He gave us back the spiritual life that we had lost because of our sin.

2. Encourage participants to list examples of irony in Jesus' trial and condemnation.

Taking the Message Home

Encourage participants to complete the "Review," "Looking Ahead," and "Working Ahead" sections.

Closing Worship

Dear Lord, You give us more than we deserve, more than we can ask or even hope for in Your sacrifice on the cross. Your generosity and goodness never cease to bless even those who are ungrateful or who have wandered far from You. Turn our hearts toward You, O Lord, that we may be thankful, humble, and devoted to You. You alone are our help, our power, and our strength, and in Your death and resurrection we find our life and hope. In Your saving name, we pray. Amen.

(Adapted from *Following Christ: Prayers from Imitation of Christ in the Language of Today*, ed. Ronald Klug [Concordia Publishing House, 1981] p. 17.)

Session 11

The Crucifixion

(Mark 15:21–47)

Lesson Aim

This session focuses on the crucifixion: from Jesus' walk from the Praetorium, through the streets of Jerusalem, to Golgotha. At the Place of the Skull, the Son of God is fastened to a cross to die the death of a criminal.

But the crucifixion of Jesus is not an accident of history; it is not the unplanned, unexpected conclusion to a failed mission. The crucifixion, rather, is the goal, the target. Long before, God gave His people a glimpse of His means of salvation: "Moses lifted up the snake" (John 3:14). In Numbers 21:4–9, God sent serpents to punish His people for their unbelief and disobedience. Through Moses' intercession, God gave the nation a sign—the bronze serpent on the pole. Those who were bitten and looked upon the symbol were saved, that is, healed. Now, Jesus' "lifting up" is the sign, the demonstration, of God's full salvation. The crucifixion is divine love in action toward a hostile, darkened world. God's intention is that all people be saved. He sent His Son, therefore, to give "eternal life" (John 3:16). The threat of condemnation is passed for all who believe in—trust, rely upon—Christ.

Lesson Objectives

By the power of the Holy Spirit working through God's Word, participants will

1. understand the significance of crucifixion in the ancient world: a means of punishment and the sign of a curse;

2. appreciate Jesus' willingness to suffer the pain and shame of the cross;

3. recognize the fulfillment of prophecy and the rich symbolism in the crucifixion;

4. live in gratitude for the Lord's sacrifice for their forgiveness, life, and salvation.

Opening Worship

Sing or read aloud the following stanzas of "When I Survey the Wondrous Cross."

When I survey the wondrous cross
On which the prince of glory died,
My richest gain I count but loss
And pour contempt on all my pride.

Forbid it, Lord, that I should boast
Save in the death of Christ, my God;
All the vain things that charm me most,
I sacrifice them to His blood.

Were the whole realm of nature mine,
That were a tribute far too small;
Love so amazing, so divine,
Demands my soul, my life, my all!

Then pray aloud the following prayer:

Lord Jesus, trusting completely in Your goodness and great mercy, we come to You: as the sick come to one who can heal, as the hungry and thirsty to the fountain of life, as the needy to the King of heaven. We have no goodness of our own to merit Your blessing. Yet in Your love You became our sin payment on the cross. Your death is our one hope for forgiveness, life, and salvation. Speak to us in Your Word. Let us hear, believe, and always cherish the story of Your cross. In Your name we pray. Amen.

Approaching This Study

Invite a participant to read this section aloud.

An Overview

Unit Reading

Ask participants to read Mark 15:21–47. Invite individuals to share new insights into the story of the crucifixion. Ask, "Did any detail emerge from the text as you read? In what ways did the story of the crucifixion stir your heart and mind this time?"

The Message in Brief

Read aloud this section. Take a few minutes (as time permits) to review the previous two sessions on the events of Maundy Thursday and Jesus' trials.

Working with the Text

1. Simon is a native of Cyrene, a major city in North Africa. Simon is likely a Jew, who had come to Jerusalem for the Passover. Simon is, in fact, an innocent bystander, who may have stopped for a moment to notice the commotion or procession. He may have been pressed into service because Jesus fell and was unable—for a moment—to stand and resume the walk. Carrying Jesus' cross is obviously a hardship for Simon, as he is subjected to pain and mistreatment from the Roman soldiers. Years later, if Simon and his family became believers in Jesus (as Mark 15:21 implies), carrying Jesus' cross would have been regarded as a tremendous privilege.

2. The Place of the Skull may describe the physical features of the area (e.g., the facade of a hill in the shape of a skull) or its routine use (e.g., in executions).

3. Jesus is offered "wine mixed with myrrh" (Mark 15:23), a blend of intoxicants and gum resin to alleviate suffering and extreme pain (see Proverbs 31:6). Jesus refuses, however, to drink the mixture, thus bearing the full brunt of the punishment. Jesus is stripped, fastened to the crossbar, and hoisted up to the top of the wooden scaffold. By custom, the soldiers "inherit" the victim's clothing. For amusement, and to pass the time, the soldiers gamble—casting lots has both a sacred and secular context—for the garments, belt, and sandals. (St. John mentions the seamless garment, a valuable "prize"; see John 19:23–24). In truth, though, they fulfill the words of the Scriptures: "They divide My garments among them and cast lots for My clothing" (Psalm 22:18).

4. The two robbers were evidently looking for an earthly, political kingdom. They may have been associated with the Zealots. Jesus, in contrast, was establishing a spiritual kingdom—the kingdom of God—through His death. The "criminals," whose brief dialog with Jesus is recorded only by Luke (23:39–43), were predicted by the prophet Isaiah (53:12). The mocking of the crowds and the religious leaders also fulfills an ancient prophecy (Psalm 22:7–8). While on the cross, Jesus spoke seven times. His first words were not a curse on His enemies but a prayer for God's forgiveness: "Father, forgive them, for they do not know what they are doing" (Luke 23:34).

5. Many people in Jerusalem would have thought that the darkness was a sign of judgment (darkness was one of the plagues God inflicted on Egypt; Exodus 10:21–22) or a sign of the last days (Isaiah 13:9–11; Amos 8:9–10). They may have been frightened and moved to repentance, or they may have thought it was God's judgment on Jesus. As a symbol of God's wrath, the darkness does cover the land. But the curse falls on the Son of God, who suffers condemnation on behalf of sinful human beings. Jesus' cry reveals that He experienced the darkness of separation from God—the separation we deserved because of our sin.

6. Some people thought Jesus was calling Elijah because the Aramaic "Eloi" ("My God") sounds similar to the Old Testament prophet's name. The book of Malachi promised that Elijah would come to prepare God's people for His coming. In truth, however, John the Baptist was the forerunner, the Elijah, who prepared the way for salvation in Jesus.

7. The open heaven at Jesus' baptism is a sign of the work of the triune God—Father, Son, and Holy Spirit—in the Messiah's public ministry. The fact that heaven is open reveals that God has come to earth in the person of Jesus; His mission, then, is not the mission of an ordinary man, but of God Himself. The torn curtain signifies that once more heaven is opened. The Jerusalem temple had two large veils, one at the entrance to the Holy Place and the other at the entrance to the Holy of Holies (the Most Holy Place). Jesus' death splits the veil in front of the *inner* sanctuary, thus opening a new and eternal way to the Father (see Exodus 26:31–34; Hebrews 9:11–12).

8. The Roman centurion remains at the cross. As commander of a hundred men, the centurion was responsible for carrying out Pilate's orders, but he could easily have delegated responsibility to a subordinate. The fact that he stayed through the execution attests that he was deeply moved by Jesus' example on the cross and may have embraced Judaism and secretly believed in Jesus. His statement can be interpreted in two ways: that Jesus is the Son of God, that is, the promised Messiah of Israel, or that Jesus was favored by the pagan (Roman) god(s) by His noble death. The centurion's response is ironic, perhaps, in that he—a Roman soldier—confesses Jesus when His own people and disciples have forsaken and killed Him. The women who followed Jesus from Galilee watched the crucifixion from "a distance" (Mark 15:40). These women were instrumental in providing for the Master and the Twelve during Jesus' ministry. They were also faithful disciples.

Applying the Message

1. Encourage participants to reflect on the human needs either expressed or implied in Jesus' statements on the cross. Then focus on how Jesus demonstrates His love and compassion in each statement.

a. *"Father, forgive them, for they do not know what they are doing"* *(Luke 23:34).* Our need is forgiveness; we are separated from God because of our sin, disobedience, and rebellion. Jesus dies as the sin payment; He reconciles us to God through His sacrificial work.

b. *"I tell you the truth, today you will be with Me in paradise"* *(Luke 23:43).* Our need is eternal life in heaven. Because of sin, we are mortal; we all die and apart from God's grace face only the prospect of the grave and hell. But Christ opens for us the kingdom of heaven and promises to bring all who trust in Him to paradise.

c. *"Dear woman, here is your son,"* ... *"Here is your mother"* (John 19:26–27). Our need is family. Because of the consequences of sin, we live in a fractured world. In His death, Christ brings us together as a family through faith. He makes new relationships possible, and He establishes a new community where forgiveness, love, and care flourish by the power of the Holy Spirit.

d. *"My God, My God, why have You forsaken Me?"* (Mark 15:34; Matthew 27:46). Our need is to be loved and accepted. Because of sin, we deserve condemnation. We deserve to be eternally forsaken by God, since by nature we have turned our backs on God. Christ, however, takes our punishment on Himself. He suffers condemnation and is forsaken by the heavenly Father so that we might be forgiven, accepted, and eternally loved by God.

e. *"I am thirsty"* (John 19:28). We are thirsty and hungry for something that lasts, something that satisfies. Only Jesus provides the water that wells up to eternal life (John 4:13–14) and the bread that endures to eternal life (John 6:27). In order to fill us with these gifts, Jesus suffers the pain and the shame of the cross; because of His sacrifice, we eat and drink and are satisfied.

f. *"It is finished"* (John 19:30). Our need is salvation. On the cross, Jesus completes the work of redeeming the world.

g. *"Father, into Your hands I commit My spirit"* (Luke 23:46). Our need is life in the midst of death. By dying, Jesus gains eternal life for us. By rising to life, He assures us of His victory and shares His blessings with us.

2. Encourage participants to share their experiences with isolation, loneliness, and fear and to discuss how Christ strengthens them in their dark moments.

3. Allow participants to share their new insights into Christ's passion.

Taking the Message Home

Invite participants to read "Review," "Looking Ahead," and one or more of the "Working Ahead" suggestions.

Closing Worship

Speak aloud the following prayer:
You alone are our glory, Lord Jesus.
You alone are the joy of our heart.
All human glory, all this world's honor,
and all pride of position are foolish and empty
when compared to You.

Thank You for Your cross, through which You
have redeemed us from slavery to sin, death, and the devil.
Our God, our Truth, our Mercy,
to You be all praise, honor, power, and glory
through endless ages. Amen.

(Adapted from Following Christ: Prayers from Imitation of Christ in the Language of Today, ed. Ronald Klug [Concordia Publishing House, 1981] p. 53.)

Session 12

Jesus Rises from the Dead

(Mark 16)

Lesson Aim

An ancient Christian wrote, "The Lord has turned all our sunsets into sunrise."

This session is about sunrise: the Son of God rises on the first Easter morning, and the darkness of sin, death, and hell scatters.

By nature we are spiritually dead, enslaved to sin and the power of the devil. Apart from God's gracious rescue, we face the certain prospect of death and eternal separation from God. Jesus, however, sets people free. His death and resurrection mark the decisive victory that redeems and renews humankind. In His cross, Jesus removes the threat of judgment, casts aside the chains that hold us captive, and pays the price for human sin and guilt *in full*. In His resurrection, Jesus overcomes death and breaks the power of sin and Satan *once for all*. Through faith we share in His triumph. We are delivered from our enemies and restored—partially in this life—to the image of the eternal God. On the Last Day, all creation will bow before the glory and grace of the Lord Jesus, the risen Savior.

Lesson Objectives

By the power of the Holy Spirit working through God's Word, participants will

1. acknowledge the resurrection as Jesus' victory over sin, death, and the power of the devil;

2. describe the unique ending to the gospel of Mark and its meaning for believers of all ages;

3. give thanks to God for the power of Christ's resurrection in their daily living;

4. look for new opportunities to share the Good News of forgiveness and salvation with other people.

67

Opening Worship

Sing or read aloud the following stanzas of "I Know that My Redeemer Lives."

I know that my Redeemer lives!
What comfort this sweet sentence gives!
He lives, He lives, who once was dead;
He lives, my ever-living head!

He lives triumphant from the grave;
He lives eternally to save;
He lives exalted, throned above;
He lives to rule His Church in love.

He lives and grants me daily breath;
He lives, and I shall conquer death;
He lives my mansion to prepare;
He lives to bring me safely there.

He lives, all glory to His name!
He lives, my Savior, still the same;
What joy this blest assurance gives:
I know that my Redeemer lives!

Approaching This Study

Read aloud the paragraphs of this section.

An Overview

Unit Reading

As you prepare to read the resurrection account in Mark 16, ask participants to list as many of the resurrection appearances as possible. (For help, consult the chart at the beginning of Session 12 in the Study Guide.)

The Message in Brief

Read this section in the Study Guide.

Working with the Text

The Angel Announces the Resurrection

1. The women were the first disciples to go to Jesus' tomb. The various women who followed Jesus throughout His ministry played a key role in several ways: they were true followers, who learned from their Lord and shared His teaching with others; they supported Jesus and the other disciples with money and gifts; they likely also helped with basic necessities, serving Jesus in love. The women who went to the tomb on Easter morning were devoted to the Lord and heartbroken by His death on Good Friday.

2. The mood was undoubtedly sadness, hurt, profound disappointment, perhaps anger at the authorities and crowds. They anticipated anointing Jesus' body with spices; they may also have planned to permanently wrap His body with the burial cloths. The women probably were planning to ask the Roman guards for permission to enter the tomb and for assistance in rolling back the stone.

3. The young man in the tomb is dressed in a white robe. White is often a symbol of heavenly glory, purity and holiness in the Bible (Mark 9:3; John 20:12; Acts 1:10; Revelation 3:4; 4:4; 7:9; etc.). The "young man" or angel at the tomb stands in sharp contrast to the young man in the garden: one is clothed, the other is naked; one announces the Good News, the other flees from persecution; one is a heavenly being, the other is a sinful mortal; one signals the triumph of Christ, the other signals the beginning of Christ's suffering and crucifixion.

4. The angel begins with a word of comfort: "Don't be alarmed" (Mark 16:6). In the presence of God's messengers, mortal men and women are terrified; they stand in fear of the angels' power and shining glory. When they appear to human beings, then, angels give the assurance, "Don't be alarmed," or "Don't be afraid" (see also Genesis 21:17; Judges 6:22–23; Matthew 1:20; Luke 1:13, 30; 2:10). The angel at the tomb then announces the victory: "He has risen!" He gives assurance that Jesus is alive and will meet the disciples in Galilee.

5. The women's reactions are (a) trembling—shaking with fear, anxiety, consternation; (b) bewilderment—a state of extreme astonishment, to the point of being "beside oneself" with amazement (the Greek word *ekstasis* means, literally, "standing outside [oneself]"); (c) fear—distress, intense concern because of potential danger, evil, abuse, uncertainty. The encounter with the angel was for the women a deeply moving experience, filled with fear and awe. The same response is evident throughout Mark's gospel as individuals come into contact with the power and grace of Jesus the Christ.

The "Longer Ending" and the Other Gospels

1. Verses 9–11 appear to be a brief summary of Jesus' appearance to Mary Magdalene as recorded in John 20:11–18.

Verses 12–13 refer to the story of Jesus' appearance to the two disciples on the road to Emmaus (Luke 24:13–32).

Verse 14 condenses into a single sentence the story of Jesus' appearance to the Twelve—Thomas is present!—on the Sunday after Easter (one week after His resurrection; see John 20:26–31).

Verses 15–18 is similar in content and style to Matthew 28:16–20, although in this missionary charge Jesus describes the signs that will accompany the disciples' proclamation of the Gospel.

Verse 19 is a short synopsis of Jesus' ascension (Luke 24:50–51).

Verse 20 is a summary of the apostolic mission described by St. Luke in the book of Acts.

The *Concordia Self-Study Bible* notes at Mark 16:9–20: "Serious doubt exists as to whether these verses belong to the original gospel of Mark. They are absent from important early manuscripts and display certain peculiarities of vocabulary, style and theological content that are unlike the rest of Mark. His Gospel probably ended at 16:8, or its original ending has been lost."

2. Encourage participants to read the summaries in the Study Guide and note the different appearances of the risen Lord to His disciples. If time permits, explore one or more of the accounts in the other gospels.

Applying the Message

1. As you read this portion of Peter's Pentecost sermon, notice the italic words and phrases.

"Men of Israel, listen to this: Jesus of Nazareth was a man accredited by God to you by *miracles, wonders and signs, which God did among you through Him*, as you yourselves know. This man was handed over to you by God's set purpose and foreknowledge; and you, with the help of wicked men, put Him to death by nailing Him to the cross. But *God raised Him from the dead, freeing Him from the agony of death, because it was impossible for death to keep its hold on Him.* David said about Him:

"'I saw *the Lord always before Me.*
Because He is at My right hand,
I will not be shaken.
Therefore My heart is glad and My tongue rejoices;
    My body also will live in hope,
because You will not abandon Me to the grave,
        nor will You let Your Holy One see decay.
You have made known to Me *the paths of life*;
You will fill Me with *joy in Your presence.*'

"Brothers, I can tell you confidently that the patriarch David died and was buried, and his tomb is here to this day. But he was a prophet and *knew that God had promised him on oath* that he would place one of his descendants on his throne. Seeing what was ahead, *he spoke of the resurrection of the Christ, that He was not abandoned to the grave, nor did His body see decay. God has raised this Jesus to life, and we are all witnesses of the fact.* Exalted to the right hand of God, He has received from the Father the promised Holy Spirit and has poured out what you now see and hear. For David did not ascend to heaven, and yet he said,

> " *'The Lord said to my Lord:*
> *"Sit at My right hand*
> *until I make your enemies*
> *a footstool for your Feet."* '

"Therefore let all Israel be assured of this: God has made this Jesus, whom you crucified, both Lord and Christ." (Acts 2:22–36)

2. Encourage participants to list the different blessings they have received through Christ's resurrection. Some important Bible passages are Romans 6:1–11; 1 Corinthians 15; Ephesians 2:1–10; Philippians 3:20–21; Colossians 3:1–4; and 1 Thessalonians 4:13–18.

3. Encourage participants to share what it means that Jesus is exalted to the right hand of God the Father. Jesus is now truly present everywhere, exercising His divine power and glory as He pours out His Spirit, prays for us in our need, and rules and protects His church in love. He will return visibly and in glory on the Last Day.

Taking the Message Home

Invite participants to read "Review," "Looking Ahead," and one or more of the "Working Ahead" suggestions as they continue their study of God's Word.

Closing Worship

Speak aloud the following prayer:

Lord, blessed is Your Holy Word.
What would we do in all our troubles and trials,
if You did not comfort and strengthen us
with Your holy and health-giving Word?
Therefore it does not matter how many storms
or troubled waters we go through,
so long as we come at last to the port of Your everlasting salvation.
Give us a good end and a joyful passage from this life.
Remember us, our Lord and our God,
and lead us by a straight and ready way into Your kingdom.
In Your name, Lord Jesus. Amen.

(Adapted from *Following Christ: Prayers from Imitation of Christ in the Language of Today,* ed. Ronald Klug [Concordia Publishing House, 1981] p. 63.)